A Cloud of Unusual Size and Shape

T0126119

A Cloud of Unusual Size and Shape

Meditations on Ruin and Redemption

Matt Donovan

TRINITY UNIVERSITY PRESS

SAN ANTONIO, TEXAS

Published by Trinity University Press
San Antonio, Texas 78212

Copyright © 2016 by Matt Donovan

All rights reserved. No part of this book may be reproduced in any form or by any electronic or mechanical means, including information storage and retrieval systems, without permission in writing from the publisher.

Cover design by Kristina Kachele Design, llc
Book design by BookMatters, Berkeley
Cover art: ©iStock.com/Achim Prill

ISBN-13 978-1-59534-760-2 paper
ISBN-13 978-1-59534-761-9 ebook

Trinity University Press strives to produce its books using methods and materials in an environmentally sensitive manner. We favor working with manufacturers that practice sustainable management of all natural resources, produce paper using recycled stock, and manage forests with the best possible practices for people, biodiversity, and sustainability. The press is a member of the Green Press Initiative, a nonprofit program dedicated to supporting publishers in their efforts to reduce their impacts on endangered forests, climate change, and forest-dependent communities.

The paper used in this publication meets the minimum requirements of the American National Standard for Information Sciences—Permanence of Paper for Printed Library Materials, ANSI 39.48–1992.

CIP data on file at the Library of Congress

20 19 18 17 16 | 5 4 3 2 1

For Ligia

Contents

⌒

Leaving Trinity
Ten Ground Zero Swerves

⌒

⌒

My uncle was stationed at Misenum, where he was in active command
of the fleet, with full powers. On the 23rd of August, about the seventh
hour, my mother drew his attention to the fact that a cloud of unusual
size and shape had made its appearance. He had taken his sun bath,
followed by a cold one, and after a light meal he was lying down and
reading. Yet he called for his sandals, and climbed up to a spot from
which he could command a good view of the curious phenomenon.
Those who were looking at the cloud from some distance could
not make out from which mountain it was rising—it was afterward
discovered to have been Mount Vesuvius—but in likeness and form it
more resembled a pine-tree than anything else, for what corresponded
to the trunk was of great length and height, and then spread out into a
number of branches . . .

—PLINY THE YOUNGER, letter to Tacitus

If clouds were the mere result of the condensation of Vapour in the
masses of atmosphere which they occupy, if their variations were
produced by the movements of the atmosphere alone, then indeed might
the study of them be deemed an useless pursuit of shadows, an attempt
to describe forms which, being the sport of winds, must be ever varying,
and therefore not to be defined . . . the case is not so with clouds.

—LUKE HOWARD, "Essay on the Modification of Clouds"

Leaving Trinity

～

Ten Ground Zero Swerves

ONE

From the moment we arrive, the departures begin.

Navigating parking and Porta-Potty lines. Skirting the concession trailers' hot dogs.

Inside Jumbo, the two-hundred-ton cylinder built to house the explosion (a plan abandoned as confidence in the bomb grew), families pose and grin. A girl takes a halfhearted stab at a cartwheel; another mimes skateboarding its pockmarked metal. My friend and I watch, speed-read Jumbo's plaque, wonder if we should head to the McDonald Ranch house or walk straight to the site.

At the souvenir stands, there are mushroom cloud T-shirts, Fat Man commemorative pins, and racks of paperback books—Oppenheimer bios, *The Day the Sun Rose Twice*, guides to New Mexico hikes, and a children's collection of trickster tales with a smirking turquoise coyote on its cover.

Nearby, a woman beckons us over to a folding table. She gives us a hand-typed magenta sheet that allows us to add up our annual radiation exposure. There are blank spaces to complete—how many

X-rays and plane trips have I had? how many people do I spend more than eight hours with each day?—but some numbers have already been calculated: ground radiation (26 m/Rem, it claims, a precise measurement provided but left wholly unexplained), water and food (28), fallout from nuclear weapons tests pre-1963 (4).

Arranged on her table is a seemingly random assortment of things—a clock, a banana, a plate—next to a few samples of trinitite, the name given to the site's post-explosion ground cover of fused sand. Each piece looks like a bit of faded coral or perhaps a moss-covered rock.

To the gathering crowd, she demonstrates how the dial on her Geiger counter lurches while hovering over the household items, then merely trembles near the melted soil. But I'm barely listening. I'd read accounts of the bomb transforming this desert to the color of jade and a sea of emerald beads, and I'm a bit disappointed. The trinitite is not as luminous as I'd hoped.

TWO

We're standing in a fenced-in field near the center of the bomb's crater that is, in truth, a slight depression in the earth almost impossible to see.

Six bikers pose, arm in arm, at the lava rock obelisk that marks the precise spot of the explosion; a group of Texans wait their turn.

Some kids run helter-skelter across the desert scruff, arms outstretched, pretending to be airplanes. A family peers into a small spot cordoned off with iron rails in order to see what remains of the vaporized hundred-foot tower that housed the bomb at detonation—a few sheared-off iron rods jutting up from a patch of lumpy dirt.

At the field's periphery, some of the tourists walk in a slow stoop, presumably scavenging for trinitite, pieces of which can still be found

at the site. As I watch them, I realize I'll never make it back to Santa Fe in time for the wedding ceremony I was supposed to attend. I still can't even explain why I'm here.

At the field's north side, there are photographs affixed along the fence. ("Like stations of the cross," my friend suggests.) Some are hardly surprising: aerial shots of Trinity base camp, the Gadget slowly hoisted to the tower's peak (a few feet from the assembled bomb, a man reclines, almost rakish, like someone lounging along the Coney Island boardwalk), and, of course, those iconic shots of the fireball mere hundredths of a second after detonation.

Those black-and-white photos of churning light have become so familiar they're nearly impossible to actually see. Like O'Keeffe's undulant calla lilies or one of Hopper's desolate sunbeams, the images have been so frequently reproduced they've lost their singularity and seem instead like any other bit of elidible Americana. Try to rekindle your strategies of seeing, and they evade through other means,

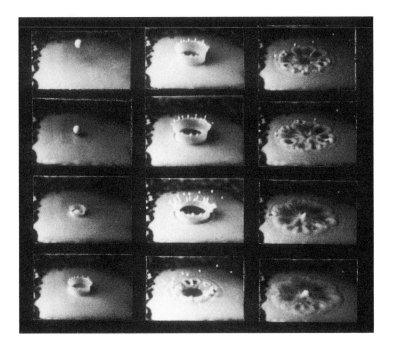

quick-shifting like optical illusions: here, the explosion becomes a sunrise; here, the fiery curtain of the debris turns for a second into the molten tip on a glassblower's pipe, then Edgerton's stop-motion photos of milk drops splashing into a saucer.

Who chooses these images we gaze upon, backs to the obelisk, staving off the blankness of the site? And, if the desert's sun-bleaching heat prevents the photographs from being displayed year-round, whose job is it, during the early hours of these biannual open houses, to skulk through the crater and place them at each prearranged spot?

Without the photos to look at, would we be bored here? Would we arrive, then ask, "Is that it?"

Some of these images, as if we needed any help, seem designed to distract from what we're here to see. One captures the Trinity Site Polo Team "ready for action." And there's a shot of men waiting outside the mess hall, eager for the evening's grub. Although there's not much to look at—the foreground jeep, a line of soldiers outside a cabin-like building—the caption attempts to detour the photograph's blandness. Thus we're told how, during one lunch hour, Felix DePaula accidentally flipped a bull snake over the mess hall; when the soldier peered around the corner, he saw men squinting into the sky, wondering if an eagle or a hawk had dropped the writhing form on their heads.

Needless to say—is that what I mean?—there are no shots of the *Enola Gay*, no panoramas of the void that Hiroshima and Nagasaki became. In the world of these photos, the only malignant thing dropping from any sky is a single flailing snake.

Toward the end of this photographic procession, we're given a portrait of Kenneth Bainbridge, test director, seated in a coat and tie, wielding an impregnable look and angling in his lap, just enough so that we see it too, a black-and-white shot of the Trinity explosion. A glossy photographer's light radiates behind him, bright as the image of the blast he holds. I watch someone lean in to take a photo of this photo affixed to the fence. Standing at ground zero, he makes an image of the image of a man who holds an image of the blast.

THREE

The night before my trip to Trinity, my wife and I threw a dinner party for a writer who was visiting the college where I teach. For me, it was a night saturated with distractions: on the way to buy last-minute ingredients for our meal, I crashed our car, rear-ending a woman who had been waiting to merge into traffic. With her window shattered and the back of her Toyota caved in, the driver, after a few

moments of shock, lurched from her vehicle with a streak of blood on her face.

I flitted through the night, jarred from the collision, worried about the woman whom I had hit, but also concerned about what the accident might do to our insurance. I was trying to measure the depth of my wife's anger over her wrecked car even as I attended to the room's wine glasses, mulled over the prospect of six hours in a post-accident P. T. Cruiser rental, and fretted over the thickness of a blackish chicken mole bubbling on the stove.

Over dessert, one of the guests, a photographer, told me about his own visit to Trinity some years before. "There's nothing much to see," he advised, "but once you're there, just sit with it." Said over the dregs of the night, such a moment of reflection seemed inevitable, easy. At the very least. Of course.

Now, though, standing at ground zero, I'm wondering how one begins to contemplate such an event. In the blankness of that space, smack-dab in the bomb's craterless crater, what is it I even feel?

There's a model of Fat Man parked on a flatbed truck. There's the striated ridge of the surrounding mountain range, familiar because it serves as the margin-crammed backdrop to those photos of men milling around the vanished tower, all looking closely at what's no longer there.

Before I've even really decided to move on, I'm following the stream of people leaving the crater for the McDonald Ranch. I'm gazing at the razor-backed mountains whose name I've forgotten, wondering if I'd call them beautiful.

FOUR

A wind churns up a curtain of dirt, obliterating the view. How can the bus driver even see where he's going? I try to jot a few things in my notebook, but the washboard road trembles my pen, rendering everything illegible.

Instead, I pull out the stapled pamphlet that had been handed to me as we entered the base's north Stallion Gate. "Enjoy your visit," the woman had told us, wind-whipped but smiling in a red wool coat, gesturing with her hand as if welcoming us into a hotel lobby.

Unable to write or lose myself in the landscape, I flip through the brochure. More summer camp–like photos—a baby-faced sergeant with his arms flung across the neck of a horse; soldiers enjoying a midday swim in the ranch house water tank—and an accompanying text that lurches from perfunctory information on the Manhattan Project to anecdotes about daily life. Some men confused scorpions with crawdads. Haircuts were given with horse clippers. Some men hunted pronghorn, turning the meat into soup that by all accounts was delicious.

Perhaps it's trite to belabor the government's euphemism. Nonetheless, events at Trinity "ushered in" the atomic age, a verb summoning, for me, weddings, flashlights, plush third-row seats; a smile, a red wool coat. Nonetheless, we read, "All life on earth has been

touched by the event"—"touch," from the Italian, meaning "stroke" and derived from the root *tok*, meaning "light blow."

And Hiroshima and Nagasaki receive a single sentence each, whereas the pamphlet's entire last page is given over to a drawing of the military patch issued to Trinity personnel.

At the page's bottom edge, there's a code to guide our understanding of these shapes. Thus the bolt of lightning descending from a white cloud forms a question mark and symbolizes, we're told, the project's "unknown results." A cracked yellow sphere stands for the atom, and the light-cobalt background on which all this floats represents—what else?—the universe.

FIVE

For its first trip out in the world, the Gadget's two hemispheres of plutonium traveled in the backseat of a Plymouth sedan.

Packed into waterproof casing, then a shockproof wooden crate, it snaked down the only road leading from Los Alamos and through each intersection in Santa Fe with a wailing blast of the car's horn, past Indian reservations and chamisa-clustered hills, past Albuquerque and Belen ("Little Bethlehem," where the convoy stopped for pancakes), past the Bosque del Apache's mud-scavenging ducks and over the soldier-dotted dirt that weaved to base camp until it arrived, before six that night, into the converted master bedroom of the McDonald Ranch.

The prepared room had been sealed with sheets of plastic and electrical tape. Early the next morning, the bomb's pieces were laid out on an empty table covered with sanitized brown paper. Someone wearing rubber gloves cupped the plutonium and said it felt warm, "like a live rabbit."

That kind of live pulse is what I expected to feel while visiting Trinity's crater. Instead, standing on the scarred soil of one of the twentieth century's hubs, I'd experienced only the throb of distance and void. On my New Mexico to-do list, a checkmark now that I had visited after many years of thinking I might.

At the ranch, though, something changes when I step into what was labeled the "Plutonium Assembly Room." Despite the thick crowds and near-constant clicks of disposable cameras, despite the three Greyhound buses of Cub Scouts, all with matching dark-blue Nuclear Science Merit Badge caps, jostling and cackling their way through the ranch house, something blindsides me when I enter this space. For one tail-spinning moment, a gut-punch and a free fall; a crime scene, a transgression.

Which, given my skittishness with words like "aura" and "energy," are feelings that even then I wanted to explain away.

Perhaps it's the day's accruing weight; or, less abstract, the accruing wind. There's the ham-fisted stuff of horror films—the isolated home, creaking wood floors, a single lightbulb dangling from the ceiling—and there's the front door hauntingly repainted with its original scrawl—"Please use other doors—keep this room clean"—as if the Gadget, rabbit-warm, were still somewhere nearby.

And unlike the scale, the light, the sound of that nuclear blast, it's not hard to imagine the bomb's assembly: near-steady hands, sheets of brown paper; a few jeeps, as precautions, idling outside.

More than anything, there's the cramped space itself—a contrast to ground zero's desert sprawl—where the mind is afforded little refuge. Here, just here. Rather than a mere concept, there are actual floorboards and walls.

In a poem by Zbigniew Herbert, a man reads a newspaper account of scores of dead soldiers but admits to feeling mostly indifference:

> they don't speak to the imagination
> there are too many of them
> the numeral zero at the end
> changes them into an abstraction

Such is "the arithmetic of compassion," the poem concludes. For one reeling moment at that ranch house, the room blared something to the imagination, insisting on what for hours had been merely abstract.

And then, even so, what of it? How to translate, and then act upon, what the mind at long last clutches? How long are such proximities sustainable?

Blocking traffic, watching paramedics snap on pale-blue gloves before dabbing at a woman's blood-smudged face, I felt dread, the vague thrum of guilt, then wondered if there was still time to pick up the corn tortillas. I wondered if I should try to speak to the woman

I had hit, then returned to tracing, again and again, the bright simple shape of the number two stamped on her license plate.

By the time I was through trying to explain all this to myself—back on the bus? somewhere in the parking lot?—I could feel that sense of the unspeakable already beginning to fade.

SIX

A different kind of veer: according to one account, as the world's first countdown entered its final stages, a local radio station began broadcasting on the same wavelength, and, for a few seconds, the opening strains of Tchaikovsky's *Nutcracker Suite* consumed the numbers counting down.

As men smeared on sunscreen in the pre-dawn dark, as a few worried the world's atmosphere would ignite, a handful of measures of Tchaikovsky interrupted the inevitable. And then, of course, they were gone.

My reading of this historical footnote fluctuates with my mood. Sometimes, the anecdote affords a reminder of other modes of human making. Even if the gesture is futile, let there be, for even a moment, this scrap of music wielded like a clenched fist.

Then again, "no lyric ever stopped a tank," Seamus Heaney

reminds us, and let's admit those few bars of confectionery froth halted precisely nothing. The plodding countdown faded to a violin ascent, then returned to its monotone thundering, exactly as it had been before.

Besides, doesn't *The Nutcracker* beg for ridicule? If Beethoven had flared across that desert landscape, most likely this story would be much better known: think of cellist Pablo Casals in Barcelona, determined to complete his rehearsal of Beethoven's Ninth Symphony even as fascist troops descend upon the city. What we crave is resilience, artistic magnificence; what we're given is a melody that, at least for me, connotes holiday ads for chicken nuggets and clumsy pirouettes in a cardboard peppermint forest.

Which leave us with merely those numbers counting down.

SEVEN

In a telegram from early July, Oppenheimer announced that "any time after the 15th would be a good time for our fishing trip." And, afterward, he let his wife know that the test had been a success by telephoning a coded command: "You can change the sheets." Simple. And not unlike the way some eyewitnesses conjured the event by also employing the mundane: *The fireball's skirt. Like opening a hot oven. Like opening the heavy curtains of a darkened room to a flood of sunlight.*

Reduction, distancing, explaining away. If one function of trope is expansive inquiry into our world, so much of the language churning out from Trinity serves as a means to diminish, conceal. *Fishing trip, live rabbit. Curtains, hot oven, fresh sheets. Gadget* and *mushroom cloud.*

Just after the explosion, some weep, swig bourbon, or howl with joy before falling, as if on cue, into a snake-line dance. One man says the war will end soon. A rancher, many miles from the site, is thrown from his bed and asks, "What the hell was that?"

Mere seconds afterward, the Italian physicist Enrico Fermi begins dropping small pieces of paper. In that windless morning, the waves of the blast push his scraps two and a half meters from where he stands, allowing him to quickly calculate that the explosion was equal to ten thousand tons of TNT.

Oppenheimer will later claim that, in the moment, he recalled Vishnu in *The Bhagavad Gita*—"Now I am become death, the destroyer of worlds"—and yet gives credit for the morning's best line to a back-slapping Kenneth Bainbridge: "Now we are all sons a bitches."

EIGHT

In his youth, Oppenheimer summered in New Mexico, slow-wandering the Pecos Mountains on horseback, sometimes losing himself in wilderness for days. After he chose Los Alamos as the place to develop the world's first atomic bomb, he also found, by his own admission, a means to circle back to a landscape he loved. Paradoxically, when he helped decide that his new weapon would be tested in the state's Jornada del Muerto (from the Spanish: "journey of death"), that same beloved desert—with its barren miles of yucca, mesquite, and roaming antelope herds—was declared merely a void.

Although his geographical preferences were clear, Oppenheimer claimed he couldn't fully account for naming the site "Trinity." Some historians, scouring for explanation, have circled back to Hinduism's interlocked gods of preservation, destruction, and creation, whereas Oppenheimer himself guessed he might have had in mind the John Donne Holy Sonnet that begins "Batter my heart, three-person'd god."

Forgive me for asking the obvious, but doesn't the name Trinity stem from the act of playing god?

Besides, one wonders, why would anyone need to plunder Renaissance poetry in order to latch onto one of Christianity's most basic tenets? The idea is already well within reach.

And yet, we depend on that circuitous route to more clearly reveal Oppenheimer's mind and thus trouble the image of the man in his porkpie hat, back at base camp after the explosion, stepping from his car with a *High Noon* strut. After all, his alibi poem is one that resonates far beyond a nod to the Father, Son, and Holy Ghost. In Donne's sonnet, violence is the only path toward salvation, the only means for wholeness to be restored. Unable to know redemption and grace through gentler manifestations of the divine—a slight knock, mere breath and light—the speaker begs to be struck and lashed by god. "Break, blow, burn," he commands.

Now we're getting somewhere.

NINE

Enrico Fermi, who had placed side bets on whether the entire state of New Mexico would be incinerated by the blast, who planned to bee-line for the bomb's epicenter in a tank in order to examine the debris, and who made those calculations of the blast's force even as the explosion lunged around him, was unable to drive after the Trinity test.

Sitting behind the wheel, he said, it felt as if there were no straight stretches of road. Instead, the car leapt from curve to curve.

Nowhere else is there a clearer admission of that explosion's effect on one of its central architects. The mind, like the road, swerves and swerves, unwilling to accept what it's seen.

Perhaps nothing speaks more to a human resistance to violence than these contorting, springboarding leaps. The mind twists and writhes, wrenches and veers, something like a fish trying to escape what's lodged in its lip.

Or perhaps this, too, is yet another swerve. A means of evasion. Of slipping off the hook.

TEN

To say that my friend and I were speechless during some of the drive back—both of us, in our way, "sitting with it"—would be true. But, again, what of it?

Whatever it was we were feeling—awe, a whiff of terror, something else I doubt we could name—eventually gave way, as it often will. Idle chat. Antelope signs. Soon enough, I-25's more or less straight shot north, cruise control locked in.

It doesn't really matter how we filled the time—suffice to say that we filled it. We talked, stopped for a burger, and, many blurred miles later, I dropped him at an airport hotel—to brood, he insisted, and drink red wine, and watch anything on TV with cyborgs. Soon enough, I was alone in the car.

Here, I know, is where some of the numbers from the bombings of Japan could fall. 14,000°. 200,000.

And yet, just as Trinity's ground zero manages to keep the parade of zeros far from our minds, I can't pretend during the silence of that drive that I held any such facts at the ready. Our means of evasion, besides, don't rely on numbers, or any single device: the tourist belt-notch; all those miles to Nagasaki; the hypothetical months, some believe, that the bomb shaved off the war.

You stand in a field that seems to be nowhere; your mind clambers off to other things.

I'm an hour away from the Mustang Room at the Cowgirl Hall of Fame, where, over applause as the bride and groom strut into the wedding's reception, I'll hear the best man humming "Ode to Joy." Where there will be golf jokes in the guise of marriage blessings, blasted

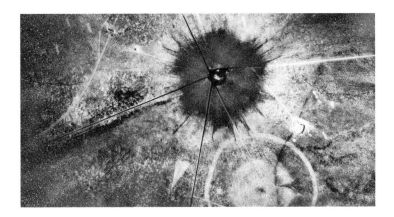

eighties pop hits by the Human League and Wham. Until then, I have little more than an hour to sit in silence, when my thoughts, it's true, flit back to the site. But I'm thinking, too, of a story my father used to tell about Oppenheimer—where did he get this?—strapping a bottle of vermouth to a rocket, then thrusting his gin glass out the window in order to make "the world's driest martini." I'm remembering a few peak-season twilights at the Bosque del Apache observation deck as sandhill cranes soared into a sun-bronzed lake, and I'm adding up, hour by hour, the cost of tonight's babysitting fees. I'm skidding back to the car crash's sickening crunch of metal and already savoring the detail of those scuttling Cub Scouts, the chance metaphor of a bus window blocked by dirt. In a rental car, whipping back through desert hills, I recall, out of nowhere, that mountain range's name—Oscura, from the Spanish, meaning "unknown" or "obscure"—which even then struck me as something that mattered.

House of the Vettii

$\backsim$

No catastrophe has ever yielded so much pleasure
to the rest of humanity.

—GOETHE

Not long from now, people will crowd the street, weeping and scanning the skies. A woman will flail on her bathroom tiles, gripping a bottle of poison, and tomorrow's newspapers will rail against any mishmash of fiction and fact.

But, for now, despite a drizzle of forecasted rain, everything is swimming along just fine to Ramon Raquello and His Orchestra churning through a moody tango in the Hotel Park Plaza's Meridian Room. That there is no Meridian Room with a low chandelier laced with faux pearls and a shoe-worn checkerboard dance floor, nor any grinning, tuxedoed Ramon stitching the air with his baton, doesn't matter. Just now, no one is the wiser, and the show's few listeners are barely attending to the radio filler this is meant to be.

Even when the announcer interrupts with a weather update again—a slight atmospheric shift above Nova Scotia—it barely warrants a mention. Soon Ramon is back, trotting out that workhorse "La Cumparsita." And if this melody, too, will give way to the announcement that a streak of hydrogen is racing toward earth "like a jet of blue flame shot from a gun"—*no importa*. In a few beats, we're returned yet again, lilting through "a tune that never loses flavor, 'Star Dust,'" the title's gag not yet clear.

∽

In Euripides' play, Pentheus can't stop thinking about what goes on in those woods. The revels, the rapture, the whipping of hair, citizens slinking off into thickets. When he says that Bacchus has no place in the law of Thebes, that all the polluted will hang, what he means is that, more than anything in the world, he desires their pleasures, their thickets.

After the perfumed Stranger—Bacchus in disguise—is captured by palace guards and dragged back to Pentheus in order to answer for his corrupting ways, his chains keep slipping from his wrists with the ease of dripping water: the god of desire, wine, and thrashing in the dark cannot ever be bound.

Nor can he abide insult, and Bacchus will have his revenge.

"Bring the torch burning," the god instructs his followers. "Lady Earthquake," he commands, intimate enough with Destruction to summon her by name, "come shake the floor of the world."

∽

They combed the Kansas malls, on the prowl for ordinary folk willing to become corpses. Or rather, to become body types that fit the bill they had in mind after wading through declassified Hiroshima footage.

Allow them to hack off your hair in haphazard chunks, and you'd pocket seventy-five dollars. Choose to be merely a mud-splattered, soot-caked heap, and you'd earn thirty-five bucks.

The director—fresh from filming a doomsday, world-evaporating device and the death of an irradiated Spock—knew what he wanted for his on-location shots. Throw in, for instance, a few scrap-heap cars, a few corpse volunteers, and the wrecking ball–pummeled Kansas City hospital he knew would be perfect.

❧

The real hook begins with eyewitness reports: gas eruptions coming from Mars, some kind of striped disk hurtling down.

But even after the meteorite causes earthquake-like shocks, the music pretense continues: a few lilting, incidental measures on the piano; twenty seconds of Bobby Millette's Orchestra thumping out beats in Brooklyn at the also-nonexistent Hotel Martinet, which now can be read, in a lowball gag, as a facsimile of "Martian."

It won't be long now. Soon, the carefree dancehall swing will be scrapped for reports from Grover's Mill: some kind of flaming weirdness is smoldering out there in the wheat.

❧

Even as he tries to stop the Bacchic rites, Pentheus feels their pulse. He can't help it. He can't shake what he wants beyond all else, and the need clings to him like the last swill of burgundy coating a glass.

Arrangements, the Stranger suggests, might in fact be made. Perhaps the king could sneak a peek after all.

If Pentheus intends to feign nonchalance—those woods, that unbridled flesh—the charade is not long-lived. Although, he admits, it would cause him distress to see Thebans wild with frenzy, he would cough up a great deal of gold to watch.

"You'd see with pleasure that which gives you pain?" the Stranger asks.

"Yes," he replies, his voice trembling, "sitting beneath the fir trees, without a sound."

❧

For months, we'd been chomping to see it, baited by teasers on ABC: one minute, Jack Palance on *Ripley's Believe It or Not* preening over a thirty-pound turnip; the next, a coming-soon clip of that tantalizing brick-red mushroom cloud.

"Not a chance," my mom assured me. "End of story. You won't be watching that."

Ah, but I knew that I would. And although I needled, pleaded, pledged nag-free chores, in the end it was Mrs. Jenkins, my fourth-grade teacher, who provided my trump card by assigning the film as homework. She said something about a wake-up call, about how—yada yada—this would change our lives. The rationale didn't matter: I'd be watching when *The Day After* arrived.

⌒

Everything was calculated. Those yawning stretches of orchestral fluff not only added veracity but also bought some time until Ed Bergen and Charlie—his monocled, man-about-town ventriloquist dummy—were done trading jabs on NBC's *Chase and Sanborn Hour*. While listeners might be hooked on hammy puns, they were understandably less loyal to the hit-seeking tunes that followed. When Dorothy Lamour began to croon "Two Sleepy People," itself a lackluster spin-off from "Let's Put Out the Lights and Go to Sleep," Orson Welles knew that many listeners, long after his butt-covering disclaimers were done, would go fishing around the dial. By the time body counts were broadcast—"At least forty people, including six state troopers . . . their bodies burned and distorted beyond all possible recognition"—he hoped fewer dupes would suspect the man behind the curtain, or that a curtain existed at all.

Because once the destruction began, there was no room to fudge it: the terror needed to be real or the whole broadcast was a wash. In order to train his actors for the moment when the crowd gathers at the pit in the field and the ship's hatch rotates off and a slithering, bear-sized thing, glistening like wet leather, takes aim with its heat ray and turns men into flame, he made the cast listen, again and again, to Herbert Morrison's radio report of the *Hindenburg* disaster

that had taken place the year before. After all, in the broadest strokes, the event they were describing was the same: what begins with the weather—"It's starting to rain again. The rain had slacked up a little bit"—ends with someone screaming about carnage, wreckage, the humanity, a sky suddenly in flames.

～

There was always something to fear.

Dungeons and Dragons puddling our brains, whipping us into Satan-loving louts; razor blades tucked into the gooey goodness of a trick-or-treat brownie; our town's cat-burglar dubbed Bigfoot; and Iran's bloodthirsty ayatollah, who also appeared, for two straight years, stationed between Leatherface and a zombie clown in our town's annual Haunted House.

Through it all, though, and setting the bar, were the Commies: Jesus-loathing Reds who lived to the left of Alaska, and who were less, it seemed, a fully bodied people than a single finger hovering over a cherry-red button labeled "Launch."

In *The Day After*, following some forgettable formulaic preamble (a machismo, can't-blink Soviet showdown; a couple loafing in button-down jammies, sure it'll all work out), after ads for Redenbacher popcorn and Dollar Rent-a-Car, the air sirens were wailing and missiles deployed and our TV screen turned entirely white just before a jellyfish-like shape loomed above the Missouri highway and, in the fields, in the homes, in the churches and schools, all those midstride incinerations—what we had tuned in to see—began at long last.

That first kid in overalls, puzzled by the sky; a mother clutching her infant; an entire cross-legged elementary school class; a galloping horse, a lollygagging bride and groom, still wrapping up vows at the altar—for a few wide-eyed, jazzed-up weeks, other than that evaporation montage, little else was on our minds. At the bus stop pine, over sporked tater tots at lunch, in any class ripe to digress, we couldn't stop rehashing those X-ray bone-flashes, all that here-then-gone.

～

Outside of Thebes, beginning to venture into the woods, Pentheus is no longer sure what he's seeing. It's become impossible to know what's

real: the stranger seems to be growing horns from his head and there seem to be two Thebes.

For a time, there seem to be two Grover's Mills: one in the thick of apocalypse, one beginning to nuzzle down on a Sunday evening beneath a half-moon smudged with clouds. Wet rag stuffed against his mouth, a man screeches around the block again, unsure where to flee. Someone from Dayton calls the *New York Times* asking, "What time will it be the end of the world?" Someone fires a shotgun at a windmill, mistaking it for a Martian tripod.

In Lawrence, Kansas, the day after *The Day After*, some residents drive around town, heaters blaring, making a tour of the landmarks that they had watched, just the night before, be obliterated on ABC. They park, and stay put, for quite a while.

I should admit that the choice to linger on Pentheus is mine. At the House of the Vettii in Pompeii, in addition to seeing a man about to be torn into pieces, we could gaze upon a fresco of a finch eyeballing some cherries, a monochrome panel of deer. There's a Cupid, rodeo-like, riding a crab; there's a woman riding a man. Here is Leander splashing toward Hero in her tower; elsewhere, an eel-crowded sea.

Except now that we're here, now that we're looking . . .

In the fresco depicting Pentheus's death, the Maenads have only just reached their king, and their work hasn't started yet. His flesh, however, cracked and faded with age, is already falling apart and a fissure runs the length of his chest. It's as if, even though what's to come hasn't yet begun, the ruin was there all along.

What else to expect when the name Pentheus means "Grief"? What chance does Grief have against Bacchus, One-Born-of-Fire, the Thunderer, the Roarer?

〜

At Camp Manatoc, in a muggy August heat, hopped up on shot-gun-chugged Mountain Dew, we were hard at work. Just the week before, all of us had watched, in the first PG-13 movie ever made, Russians parachute into the autumn fields of Colorado, followed by ragtag, heartthrob, Brat Pack kids taking to the hills and becoming the Wolverines, America's feral last chance. Taking our cues from *Red Dawn*'s guerrilla whoop-ass, we too wouldn't rest until we'd stymied the en-route Soviets.

Or at least that was part of it. Did we actually think there were canteen-poisoning Commies on the loose? We weren't stupid. Try instead an off-the-leash, on-the-loose, primal fest à la *Lord of the Flies*.

By day, we saluted in our beige Boy Scout shirts and fudged the lark's-head knot. By night, long after lights out, we whittled sticks into makeshift spears, dug pits we disguised with a thin crosshatch of kindling, and, best of all, fashioned treetops with nails and thorns, then bent the slender trunks to the ground, rigging them with hair-trigger fishing line laced across the path.

〜

In the woods, with the ease of pulling back a bow, Bacchus bends the top of a pine down to the dark earth below. Pentheus, having been told by the god that this is the best place to watch, nestles himself into the branches before the tree straightens again, inch by inch rising into sky.

Despite the care with which the man settles into the tree, the slow way in which the branches allow him to ascend, it's not long before the god permits his followers to glimpse him and attack on cue.

They see the man in the tree and begin hacking at its trunk, and although soon enough the messenger in Euripides' play will be back in Thebes, explaining that after Pentheus was torn to bits, Bacchus

made a light of holy fire appear in the sky, no one who is listening to the story will understand what that means.

೨

When Kansas City is destroyed, there's plenty of flames and tumbling debris. There are crowds swarming streets, blue sky turning black, buildings that simply disappear.

And each time the scene slips from color to black-and-white, its footage has been taken from those Nevada desert tests—actual cookie-cutter homes, water towers, and tanks buckling in a frenzy of metal and timber; pines bending in sync as the shockwave arrives, their tops arcing down to the earth.

And some of the shrieking mobs are taken from two years before, borrowed from a film about an assassin lurking in the game-day stadium. Some of the blasts and rain of metal—how quickly catastrophe can slip into collage—come from the scene in *Meteor* when a glowing orb plummets down, making New York buildings

crumple like papier-mâché against a backlight of crimson. There are earth-rending rocks from *Damnation Alley*, and, in a technique borrowed from *Star Trek II: Wrath of Khan*, some of the mushroom clouds are made from ink plunged into a water tank and then filmed upside down. And some of the ruin is taken from *Superman*, a film in which the hero cannot bear to lose the woman he loves, and so loops the earth in a counterclockwise streak until time moves in reverse: rocks tumble uphill, a gaping dam seals shut, and Lois Lane's car rises, resurrected, uncrushed, from a crack in the earth, and everything that day that was broken and rent is no longer broken or rent.

Feigned terror coached by that zeppelin in flames; government footage interwoven with disaster-flick schlock. There's a plaque on the edge of a Grover's Mill field, commemorating the Martians' landing. There's Jason Robards shuffling back home through flurries of painted cornflakes meant to be nuclear ash, surveying a decimated Kansas City that is, in fact, not Missouri at all but a spliced-in panorama of Hiroshima after the actual bomb was dropped.

And still one more from the pre-splice, pre-broadcast world: Marcus Crassus, aka "Moneybags," hoping to expand his Syrian lands, hoping to be known even more for battlefield glory than his real estate zeal, waded through the Euphrates and, in an act of reckless chutzpah, attacked. There was much, however, he didn't anticipate—namely, his newly mutinous men and the never-miss archery of the Parthians—and it wasn't long before the Roman general was negotiating the terms of his surrender. Then, despite the orchestrated cease-fire, Plutarch tells us, there was a scuffle in which Crassus was killed.

Before long, a mock processional was under way. The victorious soldiers dressed one of their own in drag, pretending it was Moneybags himself and—flanked by camels, accompanied by lutes, carrying spear tips heavy with pieces of the hacked-up body—bellowed songs about Romans as cowards and girls.

When the Parthian king, a great fan of Greek plays, ordered up some celebratory Euripides, he decided he would grant his trophy-corpse a starring role. As the actor playing the mother of Pentheus swaggered onto the stage and spoke his lines—"We bring from the mountain / A tendril fresh-cut to the palace, / A wonderful prey"—he held high the severed head of General Crassus before hurling it, triumphant, across the room.

There is, of course, no turning back, although how often we need to be told.

Cadmus, the founder of Thebes, grandfather to Pentheus, is trying to make clear to Agave what was done in the woods, what now cannot be undone. She hasn't yet tried to reassemble her son's severed flesh, and Bacchus hasn't yet cursed them all, turning some into serpents, some into exiled hordes who, in cycles of war that never end, will be forced to attack cities they love. For now, Cadmus is simply trying to make Agave see what she clasps in her hands.

Please, he asks her, inching her back, look for a moment at the sky.

She glances up but doesn't see a thing.

Why, she asks, still holding the severed head of her son, would you want me to look at the sky?

House of the Faun

⤻

In the garden, the faun is stepping away, beginning to take his leave too. Although, truth to tell, the faun is not a faun but a satyr, and he left years ago for Naples, where he remains behind alarmed glass.

Now, in situ, there's a rain-mottled replica locked in the same boogaloo pose. One arm is raised, reaching toward the sky, and, in an enigmatic gesture, both hands extend two fingers. He seems carefree, maybe a little tipsy, perhaps—at the risk of projection—even giddy to be among the ruins.

⤻

Two months before his walking tour of Scotland—"looking at Strange towns prying into old ruins and eating very hearty breakfasts"—and before he became "too thin and fevered to proceed on the journey," John Keats, in a letter to fellow poet John Hamilton Reynolds, sets down an allegory of life.

"Well," he begins, scoring a pause in his thoughts, "I compare human life to a large Mansion of Many Apartments."

Were this any other twenty-three-year-old barraging us with universal truth, we might mutter excuses, wish the kid luck, and slide down a few barstools out of earshot. But this is Keats: we listen.

We all begin, he writes, in the infant Chamber, in which we do not think, and remain a long while before even noticing there's a nearby door. Lured by the light streaming in, we wander into the "Chamber of Maiden-Thought," seeing nothing but pleasures, thinking we'll remain forever in delight. But of course it doesn't stop there:

> However among the effects this breathing is father of is that tremendous one of sharpening one's vision into the heart and nature of Man—of convincing one's nerves that the world is full of Misery and Heartbreak, Pain, Sickness and oppression— whereby This Chamber of Maiden Thought becomes gradually darken'd and at the same time on all sides of it many doors are set open—but all dark—all leading to dark passages—We see not the balance of good and evil. We are in a Mist—We are now in that state—We feel the "burden of the Mystery."

No matter what else you may think about Keats's architectural design, it's that tail-end mist and confusion that rescues his conceit from being overprescribed. For a while, we may choose which spaces to amble through; we can linger in the dazzle and gleam. But there are other rooms to see, and there's always some inevitable, unknowable, out-of-sight More.

Forget the blueprint you thought you had. There's a darkening of light and a labyrinth of doors. There's a cramped rented space just above the Spanish Steps where Keats coughs up more blood. There are Allied bombs dropping on the House of the Faun, destroying walls, wiping out whole rooms among the ruins.

∽

Stand outside this house in Pompeii, and, like an ancient greeting mat, you can still read HAVE spelled out in bits of red and white stone: "Welcome" or "Hail to you."

But what exactly would you have been welcomed into? A floor entrance of marble and slate, a threshold mosaic of garlands, pomegranates, and shafts of wheat as well as two blank-eyed masks of tragedy. A four-column atrium that connects, depending on the path you choose, to storerooms, bedrooms, a wine cellar, alcoves, a dining room, a kitchen, a vestibule in which men—stuffed from a meal, loose-lipped with wine—reclined on couches and gazed upon that million-stone mosaic of Alexander routing Darius in a tangle of spears and trampled men against a backdrop of a single dead tree.

Welcome to blow jobs, crawfish, doves sipping from a bowl, cockfights, stingrays, and clams. A memento mori skull, a plentiful, bug-eye little bream called Boops boops, and many rooms of treasures forever lost.

⌒

Instead of the marble, mosaics, and riches of gold, what you can now see in this once-palatial home are some Corinthian columns, the kitchen's stone walls, roped-off replicas of both the Alexander mosaic and that misnomered namesake faun. There's an entrance-way of frescoes "of slight artistic merit" that have become age-faded borders framing nothing at all. Farther back, there's a man selling watercolors of gladiators and the Virgin Mary; farther still, there's a ring of trimmed hedges and some olive trees in the remnants of a garden that, according to the Michelin Guide, would have been called a "paradise." There is empty space abandoned to encroaching grass.

No matter: in this house, your time is up. On your jam-packed Pompeii itinerary, there's much more to come. Both the brothel and the House of Menander are unmissable, two-star destinations, and, time willing, there's still the amphitheater and Stabian Baths. From there, as part of the Costa Magica tour, you'll rejoin the group on the bus returning to Sorrento for a prix-fixe meal, then, back onboard the *Arcadia*, sail for two nights over moderately calm seas in order to ensure you'll see the bay and cathedral of Palma de Mallorca glazed with dawn light that, according to the brochure, will be intoxicating.

↵

"Where are the songs of spring?" Keats asks in his last great poem, "To Autumn," and does not answer the question. "Think not of them," he writes, refusing the quick-fix gorgeousness of a May-drenched earth and finding melody instead within the season's soft-dying day. In gnat-buzz, lamb-bleat, and swallow-twitter across our frost-withered fields.

In the poem, we even meet Autumn herself, first flopped on the floor of the granary, then snoozing on a furrow, having cast aside the hard work of reaping for a delicious poppy-laced nap. And there she is again by the cider press, watching for hours as the apples turn to pulpy ooze.

Were there a direct antithesis of Keats's beauty-blissed personi-

fication, it might resemble the Genius of Autumn mosaic discovered at the House of the Faun. Here, the season is a scowling, volatile kid. In one hand, he clutches a bucket filled to the brim with some kind of rust-colored liquid; in the other, he holds the reins of a fierce lion-headed beast with a muscle-teeming, tiger-striped body. The child—believed to be Dionysus—appears to be several buckets of rust to the wind, and his lion-like sidekick looks as if he'd gladly scarf up whatever moving flesh he found.

Against a background of pixilated black, a single weed grows on the rocky earth they stride across, and they're mere inches from a chasm's edge. This is all framed by a border of white stones, within a border of garlands, within a border of white, within a border of brown, within a border of wave-like shapes that never end, as if someone were trying to keep him corralled, this boozed-up, beast-riding Autumn on the prowl.

⌒

Relax. There's nothing corralled.

Say "waves of stones that never end" and there's a whiff of apocalypse. Try, instead, "decorative wavelengths"; try "space-filling convention dating back to the Greeks."

Remember that mosaic was merely decoration embedded in the dining room floor—the whole idea was to linger and feast while gazing upon exquisite minutiae. There, on any one of the room's plump couches, above the cliff and claws and barren earth, Keats's nap-loving Autumn could have easily snuggled down for a midday snooze.

⌒

In the fable, a faun and a man meet at the threshold of the woods. Each has wondered how the other lived, and so they agree to an evening's walk and to raise a glass together. The faun provides both the meal and wine—something dark and earthy made from deep-forest vines—and the man brings his jewel-rimmed gold goblet that he keeps locked in a casket beneath his bed.

In silence, they pass the drink between them and sip, then walk together at the woods' edge, unsure what to say. It's late, and an evening frost has begun and they can hear the crunch of frozen earth beneath their feet. The man raises his fingers to his mouth and blows, and when the faun asks why he does this, the man replies that he's warming his hands.

For a few miles more, they continue in silence. The moon drifts behind the trees, and their legs begin to ache, and so at last they stop to prepare a fire. From his sack, the faun pulls the haunch of a lamb, which they skin and soon have sizzling over flames. As they begin to eat, the man raises his plate to his lips and blows on the steaming meat. When the faun asks why he does this, the man replies that he needs to cool his meal.

For a moment, the faun says nothing. Then he rises from his seat, flings his plate aside, and says that the two of them can no longer keep company. How can he abide anyone, he asks, who from the same mouth blows hot and cold?

⟃

Once, in a poetry workshop, a student submitted a piece about that iconic photograph of Kim Phúc running, arms outstretched, down a highway in South Vietnam after being scorched by napalm. Somewhere in the poem a line lay claim to our "inhuman acts," which made the workshop leader pounce.

"Before you revise anything else," he insisted, jabbing the air with his pen, "the word 'inhuman' needs to be fixed. 'Human' does the job just fine."

To recognize, yet again, just how snugly the word "human" fits inside "inhuman," to know that what we mean by human work is both massacres and mosaics—is this what the faun in the fable can't abide? That, after he sees us breathe both hot and cold, we're revealed as we actually are: capricious, inscrutable, as capable of malice as grace?

Although the faun's indignation is hypocritical—what, after all, are his own kin known for other than binge drinking and rape?—perhaps at least the behavior of his species is transparent: they eat, they drink, they seize any pleasure within reach.

But this human creature, how to understand it? With its baffling breath, its intricate cogs, its hearty breakfasts meant to fuel ruin-gazing? Its labyrinths of exquisite, dazzling things that abruptly dead-end into horrors?

"Too hot, too hot," is what Kim Phúc remembers screaming as she ran down the road, tearing her burning clothes from her flesh.

You are in a place of many rooms—a building in Naples that used to be a university, then became a barracks, and now is a museum housing beautiful things.

You weave your way past blank-eyed emperor busts, past a task-weary Hercules and an Aphrodite admiring her own ass, then into a room holding nothing but Dirce about to be roped to a bucking, reared-back bull, before weaving up a wide, curving staircase, slick with the day's rain, where you reach the Pompeii loot.

Here are the rooms that contain the real bronze faun, two gold bracelets in the shape of teeth-baring serpents, mallards and lotus blossoms made of tiny flecks of stone, a little sign informing visitors that "the Cave Canem dog" is currently on loan. In a room housing the countless pieces of the Alexander mosaic, you see wide shafts of light pouring over the battlefield—a detail you're amazed to think escaped textbook reproductions until you realize that the heaven-sent benedictory glow is actually frayed strips of archival tape.

Soon enough, you're standing outside the gate to the Secret Museum wing, which today is padlocked for no given reason. Because you won't be able to see that hall crammed with horny pygmies, Mars copping a feel, a frieze of a goose studying a rooster's boner, you move on to rooms even higher still, one of which contains Agamemnon sobbing beneath a lavender-pink cloak, inconsolable after offering up his daughter to the blade, one with a woman floating all alone on a fissured wall of ochre.

From there, you're wandering from room to room, seeking, for reasons you can't quite remember, that fresco of two slender roe deer that have been trussed with rope and painted trompe l'oeil in order to make it seem as if the wall opens out to a burnishing light, but you're unable to find it anywhere.

⤸

On October 21, 1820, a schooner carrying Joseph Severn and the dying Keats away from the damp of English winters will anchor in Naples Bay. Even though, due to a rumor of a typhoid epidemic, no one will be able to leave the ship for ten days, the scene is too beautiful for the men to care. A cobalt sea, the Sorrento hills, vineyards and olive groves and Vesuvius giving off ever-changing tufts of smoke and little boats skittering about, carrying men, Keats will write, that seemed "a different being than myself." In the bay's sun-laced loveliness, both men will be sure of two things: they are on the shore of Paradise, and Keats will be dead quite soon.

But not yet.

Just now, in fact, he's in Scotland, and the froth and pitch of those Italian waves is nearly three years off—a lifetime in Keatsian terms. He's gulped down a second bowl of steaming, sugary porridge, and he's hunched in a chair, writing the letter that, in a page or two, will describe Life's many rooms. But before we ever reach his

Mansion's foreboding door, before his tone deepens with the air of a world-weary set piece, Keats is improvising, bounding off the leash, lunging and lurching devil-may-care, joyfully chasing his own tail. In circuitous, plunging-magpie prose, he complains about an uneasy mind; describes weather so bleak and thunderous it's as if "some modern Eve" has plucked the fruit once more; insists that Wordsworth trumps Milton; then halts everything in order to celebrate the ragtag:

> Some letters are good squares others handsome ovals, and others some orbicular, others spheroid—and why should there not be another species with two rough edges like a Rattrap? I hope you will find all my long letters of that species, and all will be well; for by merely touching the spring delicately and ethereally, the rough edged will fly immediately into a proper compactness; and thus you may make a good wholesome loaf, with your own leaven in it, of my fragments.

Too wise to think fragments might be shored against ruin, Keats suggests instead that they might be baked into delicious bread. Then that piping-hot loaf and its incongruous Rattrap are abandoned, too, and Keats admits he's merely rambling, slipping from one thing to the next as though he were playing checkers, then changes his mind—no, it's more like leapfrog—before keeping on with his dips and veers. Just now, he's not some light-seeking pilgrim shuffling over thresholds in the Mansion of Life; he is, as he claims, a gull swooping into the sea who will, with luck, keep plunging until he surfaces with "a good sized fish" in his beak. Then he's playing at checkers yet again, moving from "a Milkmaid to Hogarth Hogarth to Shakespeare Shakespeare to Hazlitt—Hazlitt to Shakespeare and thus by merely pulling an apron string we set a pretty peal of Chimes at work. Let them chime on."

∽

How little that faun in the fable understands the messy work of being human. What does he know of our rough shapes, our backtracking and veers, all that we house beneath a single roof? The incongruities we knot together, then set chiming, or perhaps do no such thing. Breath after breath, we prevaricate, belie, buck against, renege, undermine, bluff. There's this, and then, no one thing sufficient, as always there's more.

"Do I contradict myself?" Whitman, our poet of the open and faun-less road, no doubt would have yawped at the backs of those hoofed, hairy legs skedaddling off. "Very well I contradict myself."

The man, in turn, walks away from the faun that is not a faun, setting off from the museum along a road that snakes and veers and heeds no allegiance to any one name. Rain pours down, sloshing over curbs, and block after block he seems to be passing the same shuttered palazzos, the same graffiti—*Vaffanculo!*—scrawled across the same fountain's galloping stone horse. He's lost, drenched, double-checking his wallet, somewhere deep within his map's linguine of meaningless lines, trying to weave his way downhill to Castel Dell'Ovo, the one landmark in Naples he knows, a place that, according to guidebook and legend, holds Virgil's egg, a mystical thing that ensures the city will thrive so long as the shell remains intact, but should it ever begin to crack, everything will be destroyed.

No sweat, the man thinks. He need only keep walking toward that delicate, decimating thing, and the path, more or less, should be clear.

Garden of the Fugitives

∽

At night, in the fish-light of the moon, the dead wear
    our white shirts
To stay warm, and litter the fields.
We pick them up in the mornings, dewy pieces of paper
    and scraps of cloth.
Like us, they refract themselves. Like us,
They keep on saying the same thing, trying to get
    it right.
Like us, the water unsettles their names.
    —CHARLES WRIGHT, from "Homage to Paul Cézanne"

There were always more of the dead to find, as well as what the dead
had carried.

This time, in the Villa of Diomedes, when they discovered the
skeletons of eighteen adults and two children, they found not only a
wooden casket and a string of blue stones, a hairpin and vase, wine
still sealed in amphorae, thirty-one silver coins, forty-four bronze
coins, four finger rings, and a candelabrum, but also, preserved
within the hardened ash, the precise contours of where someone's
flesh had been: an arm, a bit of shoulder, the curve of a breast, a sliver
of someone's back.

What to do next was unclear.

∽

The process of making those body casts in Pompeii is well known and, in theory, quite simple. It's even spelled out in one of my son's "Step Into Reading" books titled, rather dramatically, *Pompeii . . . Buried Alive!*:

> At first the scientists found only a few skeletons. Then they saw strange holes in the hard ashes. They poured plaster into the holes. When the plaster dried, the plaster casts were shaped just like people!

Such straightforward syntax belies our faith in acts of resurrection, and that last exclamation mark—a form of punctuation sprinkled throughout the book—underscores our ongoing fascination with the victims of Vesuvius. In an article for *National Geographic*, former Pompeii superintendent Amedeo Maiuri, discussing those iconographic plaster forms, bettered even the hocus-pocus swiftness depicted in my son's book by chalking up the site's safeguarding of body shapes to the work of some belatedly sympathetic divine force: "It was as if," Maiuri claimed, "nature wished to reward them for their efforts by memorializing their figures."

Needless to say, the formation of those casts was far from instantaneous. First, the preservation of those centuries-old body shapes required precise chemical and geological conditions within the volcanic ash. Then, before the hardened layers of debris being excavated were hauled away, workers at the site had to be trained to recognize the subtle signs—such as a small depression in the earth—that might indicate a void below. After carefully probing the ash deposit and making incisions intended to facilitate the plaster's flow, after the cavity was painstakingly cleaned and the plaster carefully channeled in, and after waiting three days before tapping and brushing away the caked ash clinging to the now-hardened form, then and only then might something body-like be revealed.

But not always. The archaeologists couldn't always be sure about the nature of the void they were tending to, and thus there was no telling what the earth would give back. Sometimes, hoping for a human form, those working at the site were offered instead, say, a couch cushion, long disintegrated in a cavity that retained its cushion shape. Instead of a bicep, there might be a door or three wooden stairs or a windowsill in splintered bits. What they summoned back from among the long-gone might be an ex-slave fish-sauce merchant or perhaps two legs of a wingback chair.

⤳

Although there had long been a precedent for the idea of casting body cavities in Pompeii, site superintendent Giuseppe Fiorelli is credited with developing the process in the mid-nineteenth century.

In the official guide to Pompeii (available for purchase at tourist stands just outside the gates), there's a three-panel drawing that illustrates Fiorelli's technique. In panel one, a doomed Pompeian kid is being pelted by falling pumice. In panel two, after a sprightly leap across millennia, there's a bearded man carefully tipping what looks like a pail of milk into a tiny crevice in the earth, within which lies a skeleton that seems as if it's being treated to a pampering, long-delayed bath. In panel three, the presumed archaeologist squats beside a now-surfaced sheer-white figure. In this last drawing, the boy is already meticulously detailed: one can make out his little Roman bob cut, the shell-like curves of his ear. With one hand, the man holds what looks like a trowel as though it were some life-granting wand; with the other, he touches the boy's back, as if to comfort this teenage Rip Van Winkle who must be drowsy after centuries of slumber.

Intentionally or not, this cartoon explanation casts the archaeologist as someone presiding over a divine and benevolent act. Amedeo

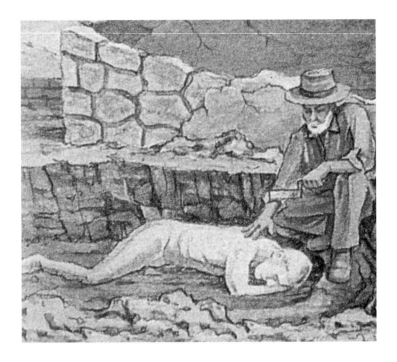

Maiuri, too, didn't shy away from depicting this particular work as god-like. Those plaster casts, Maiuri exclaimed, are "like a vision of the Last Judgment, when the dead shall be clothed again in flesh at the signal of the angel's trumpet."

⤳

In the photograph, the cast is on its back, arms splayed at its chest as if clawing the air. Because the plaster is still rough-edged, or perhaps didn't fully form to the shape of the man's head, it gives off the appearance of a zombie-like skull stabbed onto a still-hatching body.

This is the kind of terror-inducing figure that haunted my wife's dreams when she first visited the site as a five-year-old. Once, she swears, the family needed to take shelter from a sudden hailstorm and, ducking into the ruins of a home, found themselves sharing the

space with a white child-like shape lurking in a corner. She remembers waking in the night in her Pompeii hotel, knowing that the bodies were close by, perhaps shambling through the ancient streets.

My wife's fears and fascination are by no means unique. For many visitors to Pompeii, the plaster casts of the victims are the most memorable thing encountered in the ancient city. Yet despite this allure, there's surprisingly little explanatory information about the bodies at the site, and instead of signs directing you to specific locations, tourists more frequently simply happen upon the far-flung plaster forms. You'll find them in a storage facility just off the Forum, or in a dilapidated back room at the Villa of the Mysteries. Near the Nocera Gate, at the end of a lawn lined with cypress and umbrella pines and next to what looks like a toolshed, there are several cracked and rain-pelted bodies.

The first time I toured Pompeii, I stared at every plaster shape I

came across, expecting to experience something in the way of sorrow
or shock or even a quick jolt of the heebie-jeebies. I felt nothing.

Or rather, any lurch toward empathy was consistently derailed by
an interest in process and form. Each body shape derives from a neg-
ative space transformed into a plaster positive and seemed to me less
a record of a perished human being than a remarkable archaeological
feat. Instead of contemplating lives snuffed out by a rain of ash, I
found myself thinking about Rachel Whiteread, the contemporary
British artist who, in her forging of plaster casts of voids, provides a
contemporary corollary to Fiorelli's process. Her best-known pieces
are casts of emptiness found, say, inside a bathtub or air mattress
or beneath a stairwell or chair; in a project titled "Ghost," she cast
the tomb-like entirety of a Victorian parlor room with the intent
to "mummify the air." Remove the plaster doors of Whiteread and
Fiorelli from their respective Chelsea gallery walls and Pompeii
storeroom clutter, and you'll find very little difference between them.

The casting of those bodies, too, often seems to be guided more
by principles of aesthetics than by archaeology. After all, many of the
forged bodies endured quite a bit of patching, mending, smoothing,
and, frankly, sculptural methods usually reserved for the art studio.
Pockmarks of air bubbles freckling the plaster might be blotted or
smoothed away. For some of the casts, seams were sanded, ankles
remade, lips and noses sculpted onto featureless heads.

One archaeologist, Charles Ernest Beulé, a contemporary of
Fiorelli, expressed regret that casts had not been made of those first
body-shaped hollows discovered at the Villa of Diomedes. Had they
poured plaster into those cavities, he writes, "they would thereby have
brought back to life the heap of victims, and we would have beheld an
image of a drama no less moving than the depictions of *The Massacre
of the Chios* or of *The Wreck of the Medusa*." Putting aside Beulé's wish-

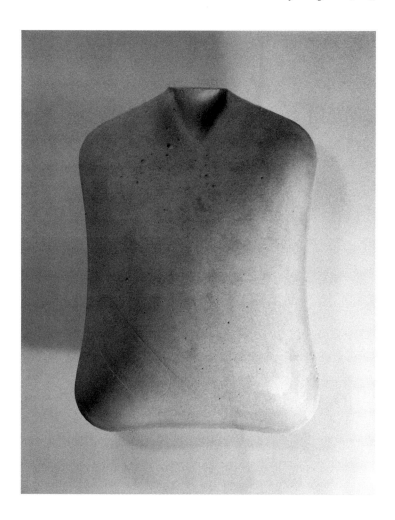

ful thinking regarding the efficacy of the casting process, it's worth noting that his frustration and grief is linked to the world of art: we lost a potential masterpiece, he seems to complain, a moving artistic tableau.

Since Beulé brings it up, it also seems worth asking: to what extent *is* Géricault's tour-de-force shipwreck emotionally stirring?

Although the artist based his painting on an actual incident that had taken place just two years before, Géricault spent months tinkering with his composition, rearranging and positioning bodies with less regard for historical detail than for the compositional needs of his canvas. A corpse's leg, for instance, is employed as a means of guiding the viewer's eye; the lifeless, salt-caked body of a boy serves as the base of one of the painting's compositional triangles.

Fiorelli also understood the potential of orchestrating drama. It turns out that the air-clawing arm-splayed figure in that photograph was actually discovered facedown in the ash. Fiorelli, perhaps aiming to suggest someone shielding his face from raining pumice, and perhaps taking a cue from his early studies in numismatics, turned the man onto his back, as easy as flipping a coin.

↭

That single heave-ho roll from the stomach to the back was only the beginning of the posthumous movements of the Pompeii victims. Although they remained untouched in the same patch of earth for nearly two thousand years, the dead are no longer afforded any singular, unchanging, euphemistic "final resting place": once their forms are excavated, all bets are off.

Some of them have been transferred from the locations where they were found to Pompeii's central forum, where, in a building resembling nothing so much as a hardware store's garden center storeroom, they've been given a new home among the clutter of amphorae and marble and crates.

One cast—dubbed the Muleteer by archaeologists and the Crouching Man by tourists—was apparently first found not far from the gymnasium latrines; now, across town, surrounded by the triple-stacked shelves of pottery and pillars, he squats on a white painted wooden box. One alcove over, next to dozens of stacked plastic crates, there's the plaster cast of a woman facedown in a rust-flecked aquarium-like case. In front of her, there's what looks like a marble birdbath collecting euro coins pitched through the metal bars. Without any provided explanatory signs, who or what is the novice tourist supposed to think these forms are?

Not that the site's rare accompanying text, even when it can be found, affords much of a foothold either. The so-called Garden of the Fugitives, for instance, is one of the very few places within the archaeological site that provides background information regarding the displayed casts. Close to a surprisingly chic glass display case perhaps twenty feet in length, above a wooden fence and tangle of grape-vines, there's a bilingual sign that explains, if not the body casting procedure, then at least some broad strokes regarding these victims as well as the appropriate emotional response of the gazing tourist:

> The large green space was used as a vegetable garden and vineyard, with some olive and fruit trees. In the layer of ash the cavities of 13 human bodies were found: adults, young people and children from various family groups, who had desperately tried to flee under the rain of ash.

> The contrast between the dramatic tangle of the casts of the poor victims and the tranquil beauty of the flourishing countryside is an emotional experience for the visitor.

Despite being instructed on what to feel, I found myself instead wondering if it was too early in the morning to offer a lollipop bribe to our already dawdling son. I was thinking that while the sign had it right about the beauty of the countryside, there was no "dramatic tangle" of bodies on display; rather, as a means of facilitating view-ing, there was an arranged procession of equidistant casts. And I was

weighing the extent to which these Pompeii bodies jab a stick in the
spokes of that Christian funeral mantra: these lives didn't cycle from
ashes to ashes, dust to dust, but rather from ashes to dust buried in
ashes to a body-shaped absence to plaster.

⌒

Some of the dead continue to roam. These days, on a fairly regular
basis, the casts venture far from Pompeii to museum displays all
over the world: Boston and Singapore, San Diego and Sydney, where
one of the Pompeii dead, for archaeological purposes, made a side
excursion to a hospital X-ray machine and, as if it were some visiting
dignitary, cruised through downtown in a vehicle dogged by armed
escorts.

Recently, sandwiched between Sardi's restaurant and the towering
zootsuited neon man outside Manhattan's Bowlmor Lanes, you'd find
many of the plaster casts installed as a show-stopper climax to the
Discovery Museum's "Pompeii the Exhibit: Life and Death in the
Shadow of Vesuvius." Unlike the casts you'd find in the volcano's
actual shadow, however, this encounter with the plaster figures was a
carefully choreographed affair. Following a tour through frescoes and
artifacts, and after "an immersive film" in which the floor of the theater vibrated as a means of simulating a volcanic eruption, everything
went dark before the gallery doors swung open, revealing a room
glowing with blue light and, spotlighted for dramatic effect, some of
the more popular Pompeii casts: the man on the stairs, the man on his
elbows, the pig, the dog, the family of four, the shackled man.

Truth to tell, though, those casts were actually casts of casts.
Because the original plaster forms are fragile, and because it's necessary, I'd imagine, to retain some of the bodies in situ in order to
fulfill the needs and expectations of tourists, the casts that Fiorelli
first made have been replicated several times. Thus the absence of

a man crouches on a box in Pompeii; that same absence of a man crouches on imported lava rock a few blocks from Times Square.

↜

Gazing on a replica of a Pompeii body cast, for example, in the Volcano Gallery of the Auckland Museum, just how far afield are we from any aura of authenticity, from an actual man in ancient times trying to escape asphyxiation, hunkering against a wall as his city was destroyed?

Such questions must have fueled artist Allan McCollum's installation *The Dog from Pompei*. Working with the local tourist board, McCollum gained access to the original cast of the animal, making dozens and dozens of identical forms out of glass-fiber reinforced Hydrocal. In his piece, the poignancy of that chained dog—contorted on its back, mouth agape, its front legs extended toward the glass vitrine—is ruptured through its replication. Here is a cast of a chained-up dead dog, yet here are four more on each black shelf. Rather than making a tragic image more indelible, its duplication many times over transforms catastrophe into shorthand for something we've already seen.

↜

Just outside the Nocera Gate, follow Via Roma back toward the modern city of Pompeii and you'll find overpriced pizzerias, storefronts crammed with mannequins modeling tight-fitting denim and faux-diamond bling, and a little fairground where kids can belly flop from the ramparts of inflatable castles or, behind the wheel of bumper cars, blindside other kids. And, of course, there are plenty of requisite souvenirs.

There, amid the racks of snow globes ("Shake and Spew Volcanic Ash!"), keepsake Pinocchios, bottles of neon-bright limoncello, conch shells fashioned as Greek theater masks, and plastic necklaces

pawned off as coral, you'll find postcards of Vesuvius smoldering beneath a cloudless blue sky, plump rainbow letters reading "I ❤ Pompeii," the brothel's age-faded frescoes of topsy-turvy humping, as well as image after image of the dead.

The oddest thing about seeing photographs of Fiorelli's casts in the tourist postcard racks is that it doesn't seem odd at all to sandwich the dead between an intricate mosaic of a crocodile and a wall painting featuring a ménage-à-trois. Perhaps those card racks simply enact the collision between images of atrocity and beauty that many of us encounter every day: here is someone in anguish;

here, with the flick of a wrist, is the Amalfi coast beneath a doctored purple sky.

In the end, I buy two cards: one of a good-luck penis carved into a wheel-rutted road, one of the shape of a man pitched forward, struggling to rise.

↽

The first dead person I ever saw was my grandpa Donovan, laid out in an open casket for his funeral. Although the moment was weighted with sorrow, the grief I felt was laced with a gawking fixation: I couldn't stop looking at his paraffin-like flesh and rouge-dusted cheeks, at the rubber approximation of the person I had known and loved. The figure reclining in the casket was not—could not have been—the same person who had made giddy scat-slurring mayhem on the piano, who had whipped off crayon sketches of googly-eyed, cigar-smoking chickens.

"They did a good job," I heard family members say—"they" being the morticians, and "the job" being to attend to a corpse so that, for a precise window of time, death might appear confounded.

And what about the job of those plaster casts? These figures, Fiorelli wrote, were *rapiti alla morti:* stolen from death. In studies written about Pompeii, it's not hard to encounter references to "resurrecting" the dead, but it's rather unclear what this verb means. What kind of beguiling act do we think those plaster casts afford? Although the casting process might capture the precise contours of a void buried within hardened ash, how much of the human is actually found in those human-shaped hollows?

On the one hand, surely one reason we're transfixed by those casts is because we see ourselves mirrored there; unlike, say, a blackened mummified body found in an Egyptian wing, these are lives seemingly captured mid-gesture as if in amber. And still, how else to explain the capricious way in which we moon over these shapes of the dead—posing thumbs-up with the casts for snapshots; buying a T-shirt with a crouching asphyxiated man splayed across the chest—other than the fact we encounter those bodies across distances too numerable to name. Perhaps, as if enacted through a tacit statute of limitations, the dead of Pompeii seem less sacred, having lived in ancient times; perhaps these particular dead more closely resemble statuary than anything flesh and blood. Perhaps we understand they're forged from absence, meaning, in the most literal sense, they're not like us at all.

And then—are these even the right questions to ask?—what does it take to humanize the dead, to allow a body to become more than one of the anonymous deceased that, with little effort, we step past? One of Fiorelli's casts memorializes a thick bristle of eyebrows, another reveals pubic hair fastidiously trimmed. There's the strap from a pair of extravagant sandals; there's the shape of a toddler boy.

Once, my sister-in-law described to me a moment of near collapse during her first rotation of medical school. Although she'd been worried about how she would contend with the wet facts of the human body while learning to dissect a cadaver, in the end it wasn't anything like flayed tendons or a sloshing lung that almost sent her reeling to the floor. Instead, as she reached out to position a hand of the dead woman on the examination table, she noticed the freshly painted fingernails on the deceased. This was not, she realized, just before her legs buckled, merely a subject or cadaver but rather a woman who, perhaps just the day before, had fanned her hand in the air, letting the pearl-white pin-prick polka dots dry across her nails' coral pink.

꩜

No matter what's done, sometimes the dead come back as heaps of plaster and dirt and need to be carted off in pails. Sometimes the dead only partially return: a single leg from knee to heel.

Some of the dead remain forever at the far edge of a field, and some of the dead are locked behind glass and bloom with light in Minneapolis, a few miles from a Hooters Restaurant where some of the living will go, after turning away from the dead, to eat plates of Three Mile Island chicken wings beneath a sign reading "Dangerous Curves," reminding us there is no place among the appetites and avenues of the living that the dead would not choose to be.

In an age-speckled book about Pompeii, where the text shape-shifts on nearly every page in order to allow space for drawings of coins and amphitheaters and mouth-gaping masks, of columns and shadows of columns darkening excavated streets, I came across the dead yet again. Although given how the engraver had rendered them, how he crosshatched fingers and slimmed calves and knees and draped thighs with what resembles less a hard jut of plaster than swaddling folds of cloth, the dead now seemed as we seem to want them to be: restored, untouched, asleep.

And on the move. Because of the paper used, or perhaps due to the type of ink, some of the etchings of the figures—barely discernible, yet still intact—have ghosted onto the facing page, making the dead drift among all those words meant to explain the dead.

House of the Tragic Poet

~

The audience, some guessed, looked so enthralled, the scene might depict Virgil reciting his lines about Aeneas in the Land of Shades where the dead travel over fields and the broad fields of air to meet the flesh-covered hero. Marcellus, the poet claimed, walked among them too, making Octavia first faint from grief upon hearing her son's name, then offer up coins for each line that praised her child.

Questions, however, persisted. Why would the poet have such reddish skin? Wouldn't Virgil, in the presence of Augustus and the emperor's sister, in a moment ripe with elegiac loss, cinch up a drooping toga rather than allow his ass-crack to be so prominently displayed?

By the time new theories were set afloat, the poet in the fresco was not Virgil at all but perhaps some now-forgotten conjurer of verse, trying his hand at lines about, say, the feast laid out for Agamemnon's return, how the banquet hall's indifferent flames gave an equal glint to the shriveled quince spilling from the roasted boar's mouth as it did to the dagger tucked behind Clytemnestra's back before it finds the hero's neck while he lies thrashing in a net. Even so, some scholars insisted, one of the figures in the audience box was cloaked in a blue-green hue normally reserved for the gods, and no one, of course, could give credence to the thought of a god listening to yet more human words about yet more human loss.

These days, instead of a poet in that namesake fresco, the moment depicts the oracle proclaiming to Alcestis that her husband must die. It has been decreed. One of the gods, feeling snubbed, had heaped his wedding bed with poisonous vipers, and such acts, as we know, can't simply be annulled. The best deal that another god could finagle—for it's agreed that the blue-haloed, bow-in-hand figure in the spectator's box has now become Apollo—is to stave off any requisite dying until Admetus could find someone to take his place, and even that hard-earned arrangement came courtesy of the sun god tricking the Fates into guzzling too much wine, for how else, he reasoned, might mercy be obtained?

Consider the entire sea's vast splay of foam and you'll have some sense of the distance between listening to the meter of the words "There is nothing to be done" and hearing the phrase "There is nothing to be done" when the words mean nothing more than what they say. When each word is like a drop of blood speckling a handkerchief, studied in candlelight in a rented room, where John Keats, for the first time, understands the death warrant of his cough. Or perhaps it's as wide as the distance between a myth about someone afforded the chance to barter with death and the bloated body of a man, not yet thirty years old, washed up onto an Italian shore, the flesh gone from his face and hands.

It's unclear, after taking her husband's place, how long Alcestis remained in the Underworld, but soon enough Hercules gripped Death in a headlock, then hauled Alcestis home to be reunited with a husband who had allowed her to die. Percy Shelley's body—in accordance with the laws of quarantine—was buried on the beach in

Viareggio while preparations for the funeral were made; it too was brought back, although despite the white markers jabbed into sand, the body was lost for a while and several men dug for more than an hour before at last a spade struck his skull.

In the painting that depicts Shelley's cremation, the poet's hands and face have been restored, and, not far from Lord Byron bowing his head and Mary gazing off into nothing on her knees, he lies on a martyr's bed of sticks beneath a low-hanging ash-colored sky. On the day that Shelley's body was actually burned, the sun beamed bright through a cloudless blue and the corpse was placed in a sheet-iron furnace and by the time his bones had become embers and the metal had been lowered, hissing, into the sea, Byron, feeling the need for a dip, had paddled off into the surf. Mary, meanwhile, remained several towns away, forbidden, in accordance with Italian custom, to attend the funeral at all.

Enjambment, we say in poetry, meaning a striding over, a run-on line, a distance within a phrase.

Once, in Pompeii, only a few unexcavated, earth-covered blocks away from the spot where workers, six years later, would discover a home they would mistakenly name after a poet and find within it saucepans, some rope, a few terra-cotta frogs, and the skeleton of a man who had sought shelter behind his staircase, Percy Shelley wiped fig-ooze from his chin. And there, among ruins he declared were more perfect than he could have imagined, also picnicked on oranges and bread while soaking up the purple heaven of noon and trying to describe the multitudinous shafts of all those sun-gleaming columns.

Then again, perhaps "enjambment" doesn't come close to evoking the vast space I mean.

In Rome, in the Protestant cemetery, just behind the towering slate-gray marble pyramid of Cestius, built with a bravado that might well be the opposite of having one's name writ in water, you can follow the "To Shelley" signs, then read those lines from *The Tempest* that his friend, without permission or consultation, paid to have chiseled on the grave:

> Nothing of him that doth fade
> But doth suffer a sea-change
> Into something rich and strange.

Bones of coral, eyes of pearl, Ariel sings in a song that's about transformation caused by the movements of tides and waves, but also about change stemming from our own desires, guesses, mistakes. How easy such work can be. A waterlogged corpse—because this is what we need—becomes a burnished, never-fading thing; someone learning that someone they love must die becomes someone listening to verse about a distant loss they've no doubt heard before. And a site of devastation becomes a spot for someone like me to parse through ruin, looking for things rich and strange.

House of the Large Fountain

⟿

Here, not much remains. Among other things, there are a few sheared-off pillars and some grass-covered stairs, a pebble-strewn atrium, four marble thresholds of four bricked-up rooms, some nettles and a bowing brick arch. Yet the back garden's eye-snaring fountain is still fully intact, with its patterns of stones and glass and shells, its mosaics of wing-spread birds and half-moon bands and a baffled-looking river god with a scraggly beard of reeds, and its two stone-carved faces—a mask of Tragedy, a lion-hooded Hercules—gap-mouthed and flanking the sides.

⟿

All through my childhood, a fat *Children's Bible* sat on my shelf propped next to a uniform azure block of Hardy Boys mysteries. I don't remember who gave it to me—it seemed as if it had always been there—and if I also don't remember ever reading it, I spent plenty of time poring over its pastel-heavy illustrations or just gazing upon its cover, with its mottled marble design and turbaned, staff-clutching desert wanderers who had strapped their belongings to donkeys and seemed to be on a long journey toward the title's dwarfing, serif-flourished *E*.

Inside, among all of the gauzy drawings of burning cities and

Roman troops and buff, kind-faced Jesuses, I dog-eared my favorite pages: doomed hordes in rising rainwater, clinging to what was left of the shore; the son of God perched atop a jutting clump of rocks with arms spread wide while a crimson and cloven Satan soars off, defeated, into a radiant sky.

⌇

Of course, this Pompeii home's fountain no longer functions. At one point, though, water would have flowed from the mountains for more than twenty miles to the city's brick reservoir. From there, it would have been channeled through a complex network of pipes that led to one of the town's pressure-reducing towers, then diverted along what's now called the Street of Mercury before being pumped through its nozzle and sloshing down a short set of center-stage steps in order to swirl and glimmer in the basin beneath those bookending stone masks that, it's believed, were designed to hold candles.

The fountain, strategically placed in order to be seen by all visitors to the home, served as a little flag-wave of prosperity and is representative of the kind of showy garden ornament that was fashionable in the years before Pompeii was destroyed. It is, one early visitor to the excavated site wrote, much more a novelty than a thing of beauty. For one thing, the fountain's positioning within its covered structure—known as an aedicule, or "little temple"—is lopsided and askew. Even more noticeably, the mosaic's fragments of stone and glass are arranged haphazardly, although this appears to have been intentional, with the irregular angles and jagged shapes serving to refract the candlelight that would have spilled from the mouths and eyes of Tragedy and Hercules and created an effect that was either a picturesque shimmer or, as some have guessed, something fairly ghastly.

⌇

Hercules—as a Roman god of victory, fecundity, and commercial success—can be found throughout Pompeii. In the town's homes, gardens, baths, and shops, he's often immediately identifiable by his trademark club or lion-skin cape or some shorthand version of one of his twelve labors: wrestling a three-headed dog, say, or

shouldering the weight of the world while en route to the golden apples.

Other times, stripped of signifiers, things are less clear. One fresco perhaps shows Hercules freeing Theseus from the Underworld, although the image might instead depict a gaggle of musicians and mimes—we can't be sure. That almost featureless head perched high on the Porta di Nola arch belongs to either Hercules or Minerva.

The man asleep beneath the cypress, or the drunk trying to aim his piss, or the hunched figure leading a pig to slaughter—they all might be Hercules, as some have claimed, but look as if they could represent nearly anyone at all.

∽

"Split a piece of wood," the Gospel of Thomas claims, "and I am there. Lift a stone and you will find me."

Of course, he's been found elsewhere too. A slice of toast, a bathroom tile, a rusted-out cast iron pan. Drywall splotches, plywood grain, soap scum, ketchup, an MRI. There's Jesus in the bark of the storm-ravaged oak, in the butthole of a poodle named Carmi.

Years ago, cued by a viewing of *The Greatest Story Ever Told* (at a time when a white-robed Max von Sydow hovering climatically in the clouds answered everything I might ask), I once swore to my parents that I could see a groomed, kernel-eyed head of the Son of God nestled at the bottom of my popcorn bowl.

On the garden's back wall, against a backdrop of yellow and blue, as a means of creating a sense of lushness that went on and on, there had been frescoes of myrtle trees, oleander and lavender, as well as some heron-like birds hunting lizards behind a painted lattice fence. Oddly, despite the pains taken to create that illusion of paradise-thick foliage, the trompe l'oeil effect was undercut by a separate hunting scene—men chasing after a boar—painted toward the top of the bricks. This is not a lush paradise, the presence of those men with spears insisted, but merely a wall.

Which is all that we see today. That painted garden began to collapse not long after the house was excavated, and the fresco is documented only through nineteenth-century etchings. Even if, just a few years back, some leaves flecked with red flowers still remained, now there's nothing left but a few blotchy pink streaks, and that last holdout bush has vanished.

In the center of a courtyard in Rome, where one can sip cappuccinos or Sardinian wine while watching wall-cloaking jasmine shape-shift in the wind, there's a fountain with a statue of Hercules strangling a serpent. He's perched on a little platform just above a wider circle of six Silenus heads spouting water into a larger pool that's surrounded

in turn by six gurgling mouths that look as if they belong to either wolves or dragons, which circle a still-wider urn-shaped basin that rests in a pool where water bubbles and ripples night and day.

Here, the half-god hero is nothing more a chubby infant, and even as the snake coils around his forearms and legs, even as water squirts from the forked tongue that juts from its splayed mouth and algae coats the lion skin draped across his back, the kid seems worry-free. With one foot resting on his little bronze toes and the fat-folds of his metal belly glistening, he even looks bemused.

In most versions of the story, Hercules skins the Nemean lion upon completing the first of his labors, impossible feats assigned to him as a means of atoning for the murder of his wife and sons. This fountain's jumble of chronology, though, is easy enough to overlook. I assume the sculptor needed the lion hide as a signifier in order for his work to avoid the appearance of depicting some random,

cast-bronze kid smirking while strangling a snake. The artist, too, must have assumed that we'd all understand well enough that the slaughter is still to come.

∽

From "rock" we get to "heaven." How does this happen? We can't be entirely sure, although some believe the trail can be traced. Somewhere within the Indo-European roots, it began with *ak*, meaning "sharp" or "edge," which, at some point along its lurching etymological path, hitched itself to "men," giving us *akman*, meaning "sharp stone" or "sharp stone used as a tool," then both "hammer" and "the stony vault of heaven."

Do I know this to be true? I don't, but I wish it deeply.

∽

Although George Stevens scouted for locations all through the Middle East (stopping along the way to consult with both the pope and Israel's prime minister), those particular rocks and peaks didn't seem sublime enough to serve as a backdrop for the life of Jesus. Thus, even though he would need to air-freight backdrop palms and his film's budget bloated out of the gate, Stevens decided to film *The Greatest Story Ever Told* in the western United States.

Meaning Nevada's Pyramid Lake became the Sea of Galilee, and Moab was the location of the Sermon on the Mount, and Jesus wandered Death Valley for forty days and nights, and Mary and Joseph rode donkeyback through miles of unmistakable American landscape against Technicolor blue. And meaning, as the production dragged on into winter, the crew needed to shovel snow from the set and blowtorch the icy rocks outside of Lazarus' home, and walk-ons were baptized in the Colorado River while wearing wetsuits hidden beneath togas, and the winter-bleached canyons were spray-painted yellow and pink in order to create a cascade of lilies of the field.

For the engineers of Lake Powell, it also meant that the flooding of Glen Canyon would have to wait until Stevens hauled away his helicopters, rented camels, and mess hall tents. When at last the Holy Land became mere rocks yet again and the water's flow could begin, the flooding lasted for seventeen years, at some point spanning the canyon floor, at some point reaching the faux-Jerusalem walls, which, having been discarded by the film crew, eventually sagged, toppled, and slowly decayed, at last fully submerged.

During the weeks leading up to my family's trip to Pompeii, there were inevitable questions from our five-year-old son.

What do we do if the volcano erupts? How will we get away in time? How do you know it won't wake up? Was everyone who died there bad?

I told him about seismographs, scientists keeping watch, how our rented car—*badabing!*—would outrace the lava and carry us home. Choosing to stopper up all kinds of thoughts (back then Cyrus still slept in "Justice Served!" Batman pajamas), I told him there was just no way. Easy.

Easy enough, too, not to mention the unconsoling facts from March 18, 1944, the last time Vesuvius erupted. During that spring of the war, American pilots stationed near Salerno first heard a sound like a detonating bomb. By Sunday night, according to one diary, "the roars became more frequent, and grumbled like a lion." All during the night, streams of fire shot into the air, and although hardly anyone was killed, the wings of some of the grounded bombers melted in the heat. The earth bellowed, someone wrote, and Vesuvius panted like someone gasping for breath and black stones pounded the trees and tents and, on the night in which nearly everyone in the end was safe, the whole world seemed aflame.

In 1980 an earthquake destroyed part of a bakery as well as the roof of the House of the Labyrinth and forced a complex support grid to be propped against walls throughout the site. During one especially soggy October, a flash flood raced through the Villa of Diomedes, causing a large chunk of wall to topple off. At the House of the Moralist and the House of the Chaste Lovers, garden walls caved in, and, on a beautiful autumn day, in a Pompeii house known for its sumptuous outdoor space, a pillar thudded into the grass without warning.

Just a few years ago, much of the House of the Gladiators crumbled to the ground, turning it into a road-blocking mound of rubble. Although the house had been damaged before (during the bombing campaigns of World War II, frescoes depicting winged, shield-wielding Victories were forever lost), it had remained essentially intact. Now, though, this place—a kind of barracks where gladiators once scribbled graffiti on the walls ("On April 19th I baked bread") and trained with spears and nooses for battles that, as one ancient advertisement boasted, would take place "without interval"—remains an out-of-bounds heap of earth and stones.

〜

In the back corner of our two acres in New Mexico, there's a lumpy cluster of rocks, perhaps twenty feet across. Because of the land's odd undulations and lack of clear landmarks within its desert scrub, I never seem to reach the spot by the same path. Nonetheless, after a short, disorienting stroll, they're always there.

Standing on those rocks, I can see paddle cactus, yucca, wilted mistletoe, and drought-stunted pines. At the base of the steep outcrop, there's a long-toppled piñon, guarded by a straight-backed juniper and a single clump of desert marigold. Across the dried-up riverbed, there's a gnarled squiggle of tree roots where the earth has eroded, and the rocks themselves are scattered with pinecones and blotched with lichen that's charcoal black.

Some days, I drift there just to sit alone and feel the sun's heat and listen to the hodgepodge of sounds: mostly the interstate or a distant jet's roar, but sometimes a grasshopper's whirring leap or a towhee's two-chirps-then-wild-trill cry. More often, though, rather than carving out moments of rarefied hush, I'm there with my wife and sons, swapping on-the-spot tales. "The Story Rocks," Cyrus dubbed them a few years back, and if our family has anything resembling a Sabbath ritual, it is this: some Sundays, when there's no playdate scheduled and the weather is fine and one of us happens to think of it, the family pilgrimages here with root beers and little Ziplocs of snacks and takes turns making things up.

To be clear, most of what we spin is fairly forgettable stuff: riffs on magic sneakers or talking ducks or a clumsy astronaut bear. Once, however, we tag-teamed our way through the lab-blast origins of The Cactus, a green-spandex-wearing do-gooder who can shoot spines from his chest and hands.

Our invented hero has remained a family fixture ever since. In the pre-noon heat, sprawled on our backs with Cheetos breath, we still find new ways for The Cactus to go *mano a mano* with his dreaded arch-nemesis, The Porcupine, before sealing his inevitable victory with a trademark loop-de-loop beneath the light of yet another full moon.

∽

Even if the story of Hercules is chock-full of change, some transformations, it would seem, make for better art.

Herculean narratives not depicted by the Romans include the story of Hera, who, after trying to prevent the bastard half-god from entering the world, transfigured Galanthis, the midwife who helped deliver the newbie hero safely into the world, into a skittering weasel. Or there's Hercules' mother, long after the mortal half of her son has died, clasping the severed head of Eurystheus, the man who had imposed the twelve labors, and gouging out its eyes with a hairpin before watching the head shrivel, some said, into a shape resembling a duck.

Of all the frescoes, sculptures, and friezes excavated in Pompeii, none depict Hercules becoming a god after he's duped into wearing the poisoned tunic that sears his flesh and melts his bones and, Ovid tells us, makes his blood hiss like a hot blade dipped into water. And none capture Hercules punishing the money-extorting Minyans by slicing off their ears and noses and hands and threading the pieces into necklaces he forced each man to wear.

⤜

The only time I've seen Cyrus in abject fear, we were in bed, glutted on brioche French toast, watching *Looney Tunes*. For a while, all was well: Sylvester the Cat exploded on cue, and the Coyote continued to pitch from cliffs, disappearing, with a little whiff of smoke, into the desert far below.

Everything changed, however, during a cartoon featuring Bugs and Dr. Jekyll, a man addicted, our son learned, to guzzling beakers of fizzy red stuff from his lab. Terror ensued, especially given how Jekyll kept sputtering back into Hyde, and Bugs, thinking he could save his newfound friend, hammered shut rooms only to find the panting, wild-eyed thing lurking behind him once again. Halfway through the episode, our son was weeping, begging us to make it stop.

Easy. We turned off the TV, said a few words about magic potions, and allowed him to gobble down the last strawberries. Soon, we were sprawled beneath the quilt again and Bugs was back, battling it out with Bruno the Acrobatic Bear, who, reassuringly, had the rabbit in his crosshairs from the get-go.

In the Marvel comics that I grew up with, Hercules managed a few not entirely welcomed cameos. An ill-advised brawl with the Hulk ended in a tie (a tie!), and, in a notorious team-up with Spider-Man, he once saved New York from destructor-ray-wielding robots who, in a fiendish plot, intended to ransom the city for two billion dollars. "And if they can't STEAL a city, THEY'LL DESTROY IT!" the revved-up cover warned. Except the City-Stealers, as the villains were dubbed, didn't count on Hercules chaining Manhattan to his chest and, fists clenched, literally dragging the entire island back to the bay.

Euripides' *Herakles*, of course, depicts a vastly different man. When that play begins, his wife and children are about to be killed by a bloodthirsty king, and, in a further scramble of the story's usual order of events, we learn that Hercules, off in the Underworld wrestling Cerberus, is already on the verge of completing his final impossible task. Despite this last fact, there's no hope or heroics to be found: the villain takes his time sharpening his knives and belittling the twelve labors; the lion skin no longer signifies triumph but instead the butchery to come. (Whenever he wears that mane and jaws, the chorus asks, "Who could tell beast from man?")

If convention insists that the heavyweight arrives to rescue his family with mere seconds to spare, his appearance also ensures their deaths. In the end, we already know what the messenger will report: as the hero stood, torch in hand, his sons at his side, preparing to offer tribute to the gods by plunging a flame into water, madness flooded through him. His heart thundered like waves pounding the surf, and, as torchlight flickered across the basin, for a long time Hercules didn't move.

After he awakes and finds his family dead and scattered in heaps around him and his hands wet with their blood, Hercules doesn't need a Greek playwright to jumble his story's chronology in order to insist that no atonement is possible for what he's done.

"The earth itself," he says, "can hardly bear up under their weight."

⌒

Many times now, I've heard the laundry room's telltale clatter and, from among the dark swirl of clothes, fished out a handful of stones that Cyrus had pocketed during his day.

Every time, when I hand them back, it's always the same. Before bed, beneath his ceiling's scattered glow-in-the-dark stars, with its lopsided Big Dipper and our own invented constellation in the shape of a wide-mouth C, he tells me the story of why he chose them, then arranges the stones in a row on the windowsill, seeming to know in advance the precise place of each one. He's dawdling, of course, resisting lights-out, but he also works with such precision and care that I let it slide every time. Often, he'll step back, assess what he's made, then lean in again to reorder one or two, as if knowing exactly what's needed to bear him through the night and what the procession affords.

Villa of the Mysteries

〜

In a William Lamson photograph I've always loved, a man stands center-frame in a field of bulldozed, dark-red dirt. He wears suspenders, loafers, a wristwatch, a light-gray work shirt and gray pants dusted red at the knees. With one hand, matter of fact, he points directly up into sky.

The near-crimson earth fills the photo's lower half, and all around him, in signs of ongoing flurries of work, tire tracks crisscross and recede. A tangle of pines and a washed-out sky fill the frame's top half.

In some ways, the man could be directing our gaze to just about anything—the disappearing speck of a red-tailed hawk, the precise location of a cloud from which lightning burst long ago—yet his off-hand, straight-back posture suggests something else. The title alone instructs: "Irving Pointing to God."

〜

Over a century of guesses have been flung at the Villa of the Mysteries in Pompeii. *This here*, many have written, *look just here, this*.

That woman being whipped, the pinecone-tipped staff, bodies midspin, heads midturn, cymbals, and that peculiar peaked shape about to be unveiled from beneath a velvet-like tasseled cover (most in-the-know folks insist "phallus"). Among the twenty-one almost life-size figures occupying the room, there are women delivering loaves and laurel, pouring water and brushing hair. There are goats, a lyre-strumming bacchante, a cupid clutching a mirror, and, in the room's corner, a booted, topless woman with a whip and a large set of wings. No doubt, you've seen it, if not in person, then reproduced on calendars, postcards, souvenir ashtrays or plates.

Theories abound.

Some believe all of the above was painted onto the walls of a secret room used for induction into Dionysian rites. Some think the scene amounts to nothing more than an initiation into marriage, as if the connection to the aforementioned flogging were transparent enough. Or, given that Bacchus slouches smack-dab in the fresco's center, some guess the painting was done in tribute to the god of wine by homeowners who, based on the winepress in the basement, raked in a small fortune through fertile earth and lip-smacking grapes.

"They can mean," an expert in Roman frescoes told me, "whatever you want them to mean."

One female figure holds a billowing, wind-filled cloak and seems to be fleeing in terror. Yet she's also been identified as Aura, goddess of the dawn, striding in and spewing benedictions.

↬

There's a lure to Irving's candid faith. That he gestures skyward, steeple-like, unwavering, toward some immensity the viewer can't see, even while the photo's cropping insists on the span and weight of all that earth, underscored all the more by the background bulldozer's red-stained blade.

Or perhaps it's his casual gesture, how his fixed gaze—not

skyward, but directly at the viewer—suggests the ease with which, in answer to the implied question, he can pinpoint the location of the divine. As if directing us to a misplaced ratchet we should have known was there all along.

Or there's the way in which he seems caught midtask, en route to other earth-bound chores. Or how the precision of his gesture explains nothing at all.

↪

The villa's assigned name comes from the word "mystery" in the sense of a secret cult or rite. But, as confusion persisted about the frescoes' meaning, it has come to denote, through beautiful chance, what is beyond comprehension.

"Mystery," from the Greek *myein*, meaning to close or shut, referring perhaps—and we don't really know—to the eyes or lips. As in to stop looking, to say nothing more.

↪

Almost as soon as they were uncovered in the early twentieth century, the frescoes began to deteriorate. Salts seeped in from the earth,
splotching the figures with white streaks, and light blared on the
walls, enacting its inevitable changes. In an attempt to preserve the
images they had found, workers applied a mixture of petroleum and
wax that both deepened the red and added a new kind of gleam. Thus
the room's famous backdrop red is only an approximation of the
pigment originally applied to the wall.

So what kind of red was it?

One with a luster the ancients were desperate to preserve. Never
allow, Vitruvius advised, either the moon's splendor or the sun's harsh
rays to lap up its brightness. It was a color that served as a cure for
ulcers and as an enema to abate diarrhea. When applied in a burnt
state, it could be used as a balm for dryness in the eyes, and, when
mixed with vinegar, Pliny tells us, it cured vomiting, blood spitting,
bloated spleens, failing kidneys, excessive menstruation, snakebites.

That kind of red.

It was a color found in its purest form at Sinope and Pontus, near the river Hypanis. It was a red so precious that it warranted its own pricing and tax. It was *cinnabaris*, known as "dragon's blood," and used so sparingly it was once called, in Latin, *minium*, from which the words "minimum" and "miniature" are derived.

I had hoped, I think, when I saw those frescoes in person at last, to lose myself for a moment, to wade deep into its backdrop red and bustle of figures that crouch and mourn, reveal and pour, suckle and strum, pivot, stroke, and clang. To be swallowed whole by its beauty and—let's be honest—its haunting weirdness. To step into the room and—nudging the stakes up a notch—be utterly engulfed, led out to the fathomless sea like *Moby-Dick's* overboard Pip, who, after the *Pequod* disappeared on the horizon, found himself splashing alone in that immensity and, agog with wonder, screws slipping loose, thought he could see God's foot on the treadle of the loom.

That didn't happen.

For one thing, by the time we arrived at the villa, it was midday and we were all a bit zonked. Through the morning hours, block after block, my family had stumbled over ancient doorways and curbs and Pompeii's wheel-rutted roads. On our way to this far northwest corner of the site, we had heaved past the street of tombs, a guard station, and an incongruous junk-strewn yard, before descending on dilapidated stairs past a dozen or so rosemary terraces. Entering the villa, we had wandered from room to room, lost in what seemed like a ramshackle design, gazing upon plenty that seemed beautiful enough—a leaf-shedding courtyard tree, trompe l'oeil frescoes of pillars receding into infinite space—but couldn't seem to locate the well-known beauty we were looking for. My older

son, testing out a newly learned phrase, whined that his dogs were barking loudly now.

Backtracking yet again, we finally queried the guard on hand, using a meager and mistake-riddled Italian: "Dove gli frescoes rossa?" He smiled, nodded, lit a cigarette, and led us to the room we were seeking, where we also found throngs of tourists jostling for photo-ops, cupping audio guides to their ears, milling about at the room's entrance that was blocked by a length of chain.

⤶

Early on in my churchgoing, I began to suspect I could answer any Sunday school question with a single mournful reply: "God works in mysterious ways."

> *Why did Jesus die?*
> *What is the Holy Ghost?*
> *Why did that race-car tire kill two people in the bleachers?*

No matter the befuddlement or doctrine at hand, it seemed that if someone in the class piped up with that cure-all line, we'd be given a *Good Work!* scratch-and-sniff sticker and, most often, roll on to some riff on the Miracles.

Gray and black crayons to color the soon-to-be-calmed storm-churning sea. Three goldfish crackers and a single Twinkie that, from a box tucked beneath the desk, multiplied into heaps of fish-shaped snacks and cream-crammed cake: from the minuscule, immensities.

⤶

So much for submersion. So much for God's foot pumping the pedal of his loom.

Even after I finagled a closer look, making discreet arrangements with the guard that allowed us to step over the chained threshold and into the room in return for which we would eat lunch at his family's kitsch-filled restaurant—"Bacco e Arianna"—located about twenty yards outside the site's back gate, what then?

As always, it seems, there was no sense of being awash with any whole. Instead, as always, this inevitable narrowing, the scraps I have come to expect.

A wrist curled over a shadow-streaked forearm. The edge of a wadded-up brown-fringed robe. A scalp line, a leg's dappled calf. A drizzle of gold cloth and the god's earth-smudged feet. The sliver of Dionysus's flesh visible between Ariadne's two fingers, almost all of her that remains.

⌇

Where is God?

God is everywhere.

Can you see God?

No. I cannot see God, but he always sees me.

Does God know all things?

Yes. Nothing can be hidden from God.

Can God do all things?

Yes. God can do all his holy will.

Given the clockwork call and response of the catechism we were expected to memorize during the course of the annual "Gloria Dei Overnight Lock-in," is it any wonder we plunged into slumber-party shenanigans as soon as the last deviled egg tumbled into Tupperware and the adults had skedaddled off to who knows where?

Pile-on, Truth or Dare, tales of bloody hooks and monkey paws and someone's neighbor's heisted kidneys. In a basement classroom, chanting "Light as a feather stiff as a board," we all wedged two fingers beneath Perry Bell and lifted him skyward. Rubbing her temples and intoning instructions—"You are getting sleepy. Very sleepy"— we took a stab at hypnotizing Holly St. Clair, who on cue proffered deadpan clucks and yaps and a daring one-legged tush-waggling leap. And when someone on impulse commanded her to "French-kiss Matt," she never paused before lunging with her tongue.

I fell from faith long ago, yet perhaps it was here the end actually

began. Given that clumsy, spit-caked smooch, what chance did the catechism's tit-for-tat recitation have against the world for a moment transfigured, narrowed to a swiveling tongue?

∽

I've had a taste, I think, of what I'm missing.

Each twilight, for weeks during an autumn I lived in Rome, I watched starlings swarm. "It was like," I scribbled in my journal after that first rapturous appearance, "being in a sea of wings."

Yet even as I began to put pen to Moleskine page, I knew words wouldn't land me close. Impossible to capture those sprawling, dervishing, shape-shifting flocks that completely transformed the sky. When words like "wings" and "flocks" become standstill clumps in proximity to those colossal thumbprint whorls that I watched became braided coils, knotting sails, then something enormous rising wave-like, smoke-like, whip-like all at once.

Some evenings, in what became regular gatherings, I'd watch from the rooftop with a small group of friends, a glass of prosecco in hand, treating the event like a paid-for show, a kind of daily vesper fireworks. We'd croon and point ("Did you see that one?"), drift into silent awe, then pour more drinks and blurt out guesses as to "why": perhaps that safety in numbers cliché (but the corkscrewing?), perhaps ritualistic mating (in October?), perhaps, as someone had heard that someone had read, it was all about avoiding the dive-bombing peregrine falcon.

Far better—if by "better" I can mean, without really saying it, an earth-bound apotheosis—was to be caught by their gathering unaware, to stop and pitch back on a patch of grass, turn skyward, and, all alone, give yourself over to the blindsiding thing directly overhead. To every inch of rippling sky, those shapes unspooling then reeled in, clenched tight, then woven, spun, then spinning, an endless cascade stilling desire, answering all you could ask or know.

Un stormo di storni, the Italians say, as if enacting a spellbound stutter, as if allowing a "storm" to be carried within the phrase's on-a-dime acoustical veer. "A murmuration of starlings," we call it in English, a phrase too fussy and connoting, through unfortunate chance, the word "murmur" when silence is the only proper reply.

As Dante's terza rima carries him closer to Heaven, as he becomes even more affixed and enkindled by what he sees, he writes that he stared into a living light and "should have been lost if my eyes had been turned from it."

That kind of "it."

Before I saw those Roman starling flocks, I never understood *Paradiso*, nor, for that matter, the conclusion of the book of Job, where the long-suffering man's question of "why" is answered by the whirlwind that is God—Master of Morning, Father of Rain, Cloud-Forger, Water-Veiler, Lightning-Lobber, Heaven-Bottler, Thou-Who-Clothes-His-Neck-in-Thunder—bellowing, in essence, "Who the fuck are you to ask?"

May a flock of starlings backhand me. If ever there was any divine shuttlecock and loom, if ever "breathtaking" meant not a humdrum stretch of a flax-strewn meadow nor a dimly star-heaped sky, but to have one's breath wrenched in a swoop of awe and bliss, I can guess what it means to see an unanswerable whirlwind and atone, submit, lurch to silence, stop seeking, amen.

~

In a post-bribe snapshot, my wife and two sons are mere inches from a seated, laurel-crowned Silenus. Both Ligia and Cyrus, with his three-eyed monster shirt and orange kids' camera dangling from his wrist, are pointing up to the exact same spot on the wall; Oliver, only four months and strapped into his carrier, cranes his head to look too. I don't know what they're saying, and their faces are turned from me, but Cyrus appears rapt with something he's seen. They seem to be looking at Silenus, who is looking at something on the opposite wall. Or perhaps they are looking at the boy who is peering into the pot that Silenus holds, seeing, perhaps, his own reflection, or a reflection of the actor's mask another boy holds up behind the gazer's head, or—how this is discerned, I'm not at all sure—an image of himself withered and aged, or perhaps, in a kind of existential gag, simply an empty pot.

While I could simply stop writing, walk into the next room, and ask my son what it was that, for a moment, held him transfixed, I'd

rather not. It's not that he's busy (although he is, building "a time machine with a bench"), so much as that the answer would offer little in return. Just now, I'd rather gaze upon my family gazing upon those frescoes, forever gazing upon who knows what.

Not that I mean mere gazing to be solace when solace is needed most. Not that some fragment or flock should be consolation for the likes of Job. For his ashes, and silence, and boil-covered flesh, for his servants slain, the heaven-sent fire, and all his children dead. For the woman—inconsolable, painted on the wall—whose suffering we will never understand.

For the father of a friend, who, just before he died, with the idea that he might look upon autumn foliage one last time, was loaded into a La-Z-Boy chair roped down in a pickup's bed.

It was late afternoon, and they eased down the drive, heading out toward the fields and a five-mile stretch where September oaks were already brick red. Someone else squatted in the back, gripping his hand, shading him with an umbrella. They hadn't even left the cul-de-sac before the man muttered, "That's enough," meaning this sightseeing offered him nothing, and the truck slowed, stopped, then turned and headed back home.

I know there's much in the way of narrowing I haven't mentioned here at all.

⟿

After King Midas became convinced that Silenus could, if snared, cough up the secret to life, he decided to lay a trap. Beneath Mount Bermion, in a garden where branches drooped with blossoms, Midas laced a stream with wine, knowing that the chubby follower of Bacchus couldn't resist. Sure enough, days later, Silenus staggered through the thorny scrub and glutted himself on the booze-laced water until, as planned, he could drink no more and collapsed into a wine-deepened sleep. When he awoke, he was strapped to the trunk of an oak and told by the king that he wouldn't be released until he shared the secret he held.

Silenus was eager to oblige. "It is best for a man never to have been born," he pronounced. "Second best is to die soon."

Who am I to respond?

Were these words spoken by someone who wished to die mercifully soon even as his daughter slipped the umbrella back into the hallway stand, and the pickup cooled and ticked out in the garage with no fallen oak leaves snared in its bed, I would, I swear, keep my mouth sealed shut.

But this is Silenus, glassy-eyed, speaking in what is merely a story in which no one will die. In which a king, ravenous for an answer that would preclude all else, had no use for the furtive uselessness of blossoms and oaks or, for that matter, any earthbound, happened-upon thing that accrues to nothing, and points nowhere, and yet, for the moment, is enough.

Do I mean any minutia is priceless, that, as in another Midas story, any fingered small thing becomes gold? To insist so, I think, would be doctrine of another color.

But I mean the plenitude of the partial, to be awash not with "the" but "a."

Not Semele, hankering to look upon the immeasurable, whole-hog divine, incinerated by Jupiter careening through her bedroom in the form of a fire-spewing cloud, but Moses, yes, his face pressed against that cleft rock, rapt in seeing that "hind part" scrap of God. And failing the luxury of Glory's backside, I mean the fissured rock itself, lingering there and leaning in, feeling it cooled by a starless night, deep breathing its unknowable scent.

Dew Point

⤳

Acres of morning-drenched hydrangea; a snow leopard spooning the snowy lamb beneath a willow's blotchy shade; adder-mouth orchids the bullfinches never peck—no matter what precisely they're leaving behind, what they step into is no dew-damp world. The visible earth is nothing but jaundiced boulders, two pre-scorched barren heaps. And the sky is no longer a sky, but only an undercoat where a sky once was.

Because of the way the azurite has decayed, the couple seems to be leaving paradise in divided spheres. Eve is encased in a bubble of pale blue-gray, whereas a darker blue clings to the contours of Adam's body, reaching from his ribs down to his penis and thigh, extending the length of his back in the shape of a scythe, a hook.

He buries his face in his hands, unable to see. She lifts her head, eyes clenched, clutches herself, and wails. Even a few paces into this world of loss—a place she will now never not be—her skin is fissured and pockmarked, freckled with age and rot.

⤳

We'll never know if Kobayashi Yatarō considered his life a happy one. Born in a tiny mountaintop village, his path to becoming one of

Japan's haiku masters was inscribed with his mother's death when he was just two years old; a lifelong dispute with his stepmother that led, after his father died, to more than a decade of contentious litigation regarding the family home; the deaths of four children; a marriage to a woman who died in childbirth; a second marriage he annulled after a year; and a marriage to a woman he left behind, along with an unborn daughter, when he died in 1827. "A bath when you're born, / a bath when you die, / how stupid," he writes as his swan song. And yet emphatic, content, he also writes somewhere within his more than twenty thousand poems: "Dewdrops falling / drip-drip, this world / is good!"

At some point—we don't know precisely when—he chose to call himself Issa, which means, I'm told, "a cup of tea," "one cup of tea," or "a single bubble in a cup of tea."

⌒

Forget suffering for a moment. It's not this Expulsion's pitch-perfect agony that lights the fire under Michelangelo's already char-stained ass, gluing him, sketchbook in hand, day after day to the Brancacci pews. Just above the couple in misery, an angel—how could you miss him?—with a chiaroscuroed neck hovers in a rust-red robe on a rust-red flying blanket. And yet, on a wall without depth, on a flat plane of plaster, both the angel's body and his fluttering cloth recede, seeming to extend away from the viewer and jutting into what once was sky.

Around the same time, on a church wall north of the Arno, Sloppy Tom (what Masaccio's name means) does it again. Mary and Saint John kneel at a cross on which Jesus dies, or is already dead. The artist has also painted in two patrons, kneeling at a polite remove, as well as a skeleton reclining above a matter-of-fact Italian phrase that roughly translates into "I was once like you, one day you'll be like me"—yet none of that is news. The news here disappears and recedes from the dying. The news is longitude and horizontal planes, how the painted ceiling's vault ribs retreat, the way the coffering seems to

enter the wall where entrance should not be possible. Nails are not merely nails hammered into flesh, but nails hammered into flesh in perspective. Sloppy Tom has made the vanishing point clear.

ب

"Paint a picture with words," we were told by Ms. Price on Japan Day, and, beyond that, a simple formula: 5-7-5. We finger-tapped syllables, bantered about what it means to "really look," and then, practicing wild loops of calligraphy, trying to keep our capital letters within the mint-green solid lines, trying to keep our lowercase letters just below the broken mint-green dots dividing each row, we scrawled out seventeen syllables about frogs or squashed frogs, aspens or rainbows or, if you were brown-nosing Tammy B. with Harvard cobblestones already locked in her sights, dirt flecking the back of a yellow jacket that had alighted on a well's brick rim. Then we drew a picture. Easy. Like plugging in numbers for some experiment in Ms. Dejanski's science class down the hall: tallying the tiger-striped grasshoppers still alive in our ecosystems; dropping ice cubes, one by one, into a soon-to-be-glistening can in order to measure the dew point.

ب

On the one-year anniversary of the death of his second son, Issa wrote one version of a much-anthologized haiku: "This is a dewdrop world. / I know that it is. / And yet . . . and yet . . . "—the poem trailing off, refusing to close, or really to say much at all. Two years later, after the death of his daughter, Sato, who did not live much beyond her first birthday, Issa rewrote his poem with the slightest of changes: "The world of dew / is a world of dew. / And yet . . . and yet . . . " Both poems are composed of just a handful of words, mostly unvaried in English translations: "the world of dew" becomes "all the world is dew"; "and yet" becomes "although."

Lurch toward a linear reading of this poem—in which a central teaching of Buddhism is posited, then tacitly undercut—and you're nowhere close to hearing the speaker toppling into grief. But what exactly does that tumble and reticence sound like? Wedged into this small handful of words is a silence that surges and teems, teeters and brims with such stammering need that, in the end, it doesn't seem soundless at all.

"Silence is so accurate," Mark Rothko once said, and yet how different breeds of silence can be. Lear clutches Cordelia's lifeless body, howling, fulfilling his pentameter with a litany of "nevers" before repeating his desperate final words: "Look there . . . look there." Compare the ghastly silent wail of Masaccio's Eve with the unsaid in Issa's wavering bereavement, and it's clear language can fail in innumerable ways.

↬

From the back of the chapel, Masolino watches Sloppy Tom squat on the scaffold. The kid's flitting through a patch of earth, darkening it with slender bands that will become the apostles' shadows. It's all Masaccio has left today to complete, but now he pauses, leans back, studies for a moment what he's done. As for Little Tom (what Masolino's name means), the window of what isn't complete has also narrowed. The hills that don't recede into infinity, which, years on, will be blackened by smoke and scuffed with mildew that will be mistaken by a nineteenth-century engraver as painted hillside shrubs, are done. As are Peter's azurite robes and the tonsured monk and most of the sardine-packed crowd. Today, all that's left to do is the dark folds of the woman's robe, and the robes of the man kneeling in closed-eyes prayer, and the earth on which they stand.

Masolino, who is Masaccio's teacher and eighteen years his senior, can't understand why the kid, for god's sake, doesn't bathe. Grease sheens Sloppy Tom's scalp, and, as usual, the pits of his shirt are damp with dark rings. Looking at the paintbrush dwarfed by Masaccio's oversized paw, he thinks that the kid's hands don't even seem attached to his wrists, as if they might at any moment go flapping off through the air like the wings of some ungainly duck. From this angle on the scaffold, he can drink in both Eves—they've each painted one—and wonders if it matters that there's no resemblance. Rather than a recasting of the same person, they barely seem as if they belong to the same species.

Because directly across from Masaccio's lumpy, disproportionate Eve, Little Tom's made a slender, brown-eyed thing. Her arm curls around the fig tree trunk, and she lounges in a courtier pose wearing nothing but a fissure of the paint's decay that weaves across her neck like a gift of braided gold. Crop her head from the scene—just as the cracked paint seems to—and she could have been one of Botticelli's barefoot Graces, glissading across a poppy-strewn forest. Even as she holds the forbidden fruit and the woman-headed serpent looks on while all of Paradise holds its breath, Eve knows—because what word for "fleeting" could she have?—this will last forever.

Just over a century back, viewers described Masolino's depiction of Eden as a scene clustered with grasses and thick fields of flowers and hills caking the horizon. Yet all of that is lost, and what had once been a world of blossom, brilliance, and endless distance has become a sea of monochrome black.

⤺

Twice now, I've had postcard reproductions of Masaccio's *Expulsion* stolen from outside my office door. Once, the image was swiped during the summer vacation; once I returned from a Grievance Committee slog only to find, instead of Eve's silent scream, a patch of bare corkboard.

Back at home, I have a translation of Issa's haiku affixed above my

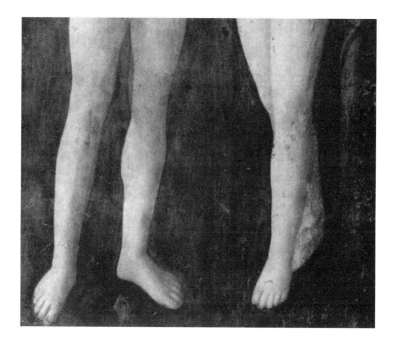

desk. The words are scribbled on an index card in sun-faded blue ink
and sandwiched between whatever ephemera once caught my attention: a black-and-white postcard of a woman side-stroking with a pig
in a pool; an ink imprint of my son's foot from the day he was born;
Thelonious Monk, in profile, armed with an indiscernible gaze.

I remember writing out Issa's lines and pausing again over those
ellipses. The original Japanese doesn't include punctuation, meaning
those dots—those breaths, that chiseled-out space—which conclude
most English translations are merely implied by the poet's repetitions.
And yet it's hard for me to imagine experiencing this poem without
a clear scoring of language's dissolution. No matter how you might
read those two clumps of specks on the page, they act like a piano's
damper pedal, allowing the almost-said to keep burrowing through

air and rupturing, in a sense, the haiku form, since the poem keeps spilling past its last syllables. And if words are no longer adequate, those ellipses serve more of a visual function: they're rows of stones or a clipped perforation. They're a fissure, a suture, a toppled cairn. A few speckled drops of dew.

↩

Maybe because he'd already tackled the intricate geometries of architecture within other frescoes, Masaccio doesn't bother to put the gate of Eden in perspective. In lieu of curvature and disappearing stones, *The Expulsion*'s gate is composed of only a slim stack of rampart bricks and a slender oval of shadow—Eden's entrance—that extends the tower's entire length. And in lieu of any glimpse of the blossomy flourishing they're leaving behind, Masaccio, tossing us a meager metonymic bone, includes a few streaks jutting out from paradise that serve as a stand-in for forfeited radiance.

I'm told those emanating lines were once lushly gilded, but over the centuries that gold, too, has turned to a few blue-black impregnable marks and the same bland undercoat of the sky.

↩

Ms. Price, who whizzed through her classroom like a jar-sealed wasp, was never above an ear-flick or well-timed curse or, truth to tell, an all-out winging-it lie. In Room 209, passion trumped accuracy any day. Thus Grant became president on the eve of Lincoln's death, and almost every nonporcine creature in *Animal Farm*—Moses the raven, Boxer the horse, every last hen and cow—symbolized (our first trafficking with that word) Nazi Germany Jews. Perhaps even more egregious, Whitney Houston's "Greatest Love of All" was "the best song ever written," a fact she demonstrated by playing that slow-building, synthesizer-fueled pop hit three times through before calling on us, one by one, to explain what the song meant (Tammy

B., chronic butt-licker, merely regurgitated its first line; Jason K., as always, pretended to cry).

At some point during the year, while veering from lessons, say, on prepositions ("Anything we can do to Prep is a preposition," she'd insist, before flinging her stuffed bear *around* the room, *over* Lenny D.'s head, and, much to our joy, *out* the second-floor window), and the Holocaust (not a history lesson so much as an insistence that we stare in silence at *Time-Life* photographs of the ovens), and *The Outsiders* (any whisper of the line "Stay gold, Ponyboy," caused Jason K.'s face to contort into blubbery wetness), Ms. Price decided we needed a bit of art education. What brought this on? Who knows, but soon enough she'd rummaged through desk drawers, loaded up the projector, and, lights flicked off, had us swooping through black-framed boxes of art in some "Great Paintings" filmstrip. It was a leapfrogging cascade: a starry night, patrons lingering late at a diner, and the scrambled-up flesh that was Picasso's *Demoiselles d'Avignon* and which sent us erupting into incredulous guffaws. She was improvising, of course, and at some point during her breakneck show, she started simply eliding what she didn't know, or crediting Michelangelo with anything that seemed antiquated: *Girl with a Pearl Earring*, Venus surfing on her shell, probably Leonardo's *Last Supper*, most definitely Masaccio's *Expulsion*. Picasso's cave-cramped flesh-jumble may have sent us reeling into snowballing giggles, but once our careening journey paused on that Eve, Price shut down our tittering with a single bellowed line: "Look at that woman's face, people," she said, "and ask yourself how Michelangelo could have known about Auschwitz."

I don't know the first thing about the language of Issa's original texts, so I have to rely on others to carve out some kind of entrance. Phoning my uncle's teacher of Japanese in Honolulu, I learned that the word *tokushin*, which Issa uses in the first version of his elegy, essentially means "I'm trying to understand." As in, "I know the things of this world are transient, but I'm still internalizing that fact." She told me the root *shin* means "body" or "spirit" or "center," and that its Chinese character—心—looks like the shape of a human heart. And she explained that *tokushin* is a bit antiquated, really, having faded from everyday use.

As for that dew—*tsuyu* in Japanese—I'm told it's long served as metaphoric shorthand for transience in Japanese literature. Almost two hundred years before Issa will grieve for his children, Toyotomi Hideyoshi, the country's great unifier, writes just before he dies, "My life / Came like dew / Disappears like dew." And one translation of the Buddha's Diamond Sutra describes our fleeting life as

> Like a tiny drop of dew, or a bubble floating in a stream;
> Like a flash of lightning in a summer cloud,
> Or a flickering lamp, an illusion, a phantom, or a dream.

And yet Issa, forgoing list-making, tenaciously adheres to dew in both of these elegies. Not that this word, used by him in over seventy different haikus, is employed in any formulaic way. "Sloppy, yes," Issa writes in one poem, "but the dewdrops are pearls, / pearls!" insisting on dew as tangible treasure, repeating words out of exuberance rather than grief. And dew, although fleeting, loans the world a radiant glistening. Think of Keats's dew-showers in *Endymion* that drench the sight, bathe the spirit, and create a "breathless honey-feel of bliss."

༒

Go see the Brancacci frescoes in Florence, and you'll suffer long lines and heat. You'll fork over four euros and, waiting for your ticket group to be ushered in, kill time in the gift shop (*Expulsion* stationery, Caravaggio tote bags) now attached to the thirteenth-century church. You might watch the informational video that explains how Masaccio's frescoes explore "the mystery of salvation" before reenacting the chapel's 1771 fire with lapping, computer-generated flames. You're probably wired on overpriced espressos, you may be bloated with a triple-scoop mistake of grapefruit-champagne gelato, but, when your group is summoned, you'll go. You'll be told, repeatedly, "No flash, no flash." You'll have fifteen minutes to look.

Because I had only seen reproductions of individual fresco panels before visiting Tuscany, I'd always imagined those brightly lit moments would be thoughtfully spaced, floating on gel packs of white wall. Nothing prepared me, then, for that onslaught of pigment when I first stepped into one of those crammed little chapels. To say one is "enveloped" by color connotes a coddling and benevolence far from the mark. For those first few moments, before you find a foothold and willfully slow your flittering eyes, you're bombarded by crucifixions, leafy shrubs, stone buildings and arches and stylized hands and fold upon fold of bright, monochrome robes. For a moment, the world's every square inch teems in an impossible bustle and you hyperventilate color.

Then I found her: top panel, far left.

I remember standing there, head cocked back, both seeing her and not seeing her at all. Confrontations by original artwork, especially when the image has been thoroughly appropriated as a cultural icon, require strategic reconstitutions of seeing. In Chicago, for instance, standing a few feet from the dour, oval-headed farmers of *American Gothic*, I found myself, as a means of trying to see what was directly in front of me, seeking out portions of the painting—canary-yellow stains on his overalls; potted hollyhocks on the background home's porch—perhaps not conveyed by shorthand parodies found in everything from Peewee's Playhouse to Paul Newman salad dressing. But

I was sharing that packed space with other photo-snapping tourists ("No flash!") and languages collided in a hushed, steady drone and she towered perhaps ten or twelve feet above me, making the vantage point for "really looking" all wrong.

Nonetheless, I cocked my head back, trying to narrow my world to only this weeping Eve. Yet Adam weeps too, and that foreshortened rust-cloaked angel recedes, and Peter, lakeside, squats a few inches away, rummaging in a fish, apparently looking for a coin. I stared anyway, trying to momentarily inhabit her skin or to lose myself in the black of her gaping mouth. Nothing worked.

When I look at close-up reproductions of Masaccio's Eve now, I see that her open mouth isn't filled with a pure black at all. Instead, there's a brush-stroked swirl of gradations—a brownish darkness, yes, but also something of the blaring light she's stepping toward, something of the ochre that comprises her flesh.

Even within all the wadded-up wrongness of my teacher linking her omnipresent Michelangelo to the Holocaust—forgive me—I take her point. Wacky crackpot though she might have been, Ms. Price saw in that rendering of Eve's face a timelessness that, at least in its reproductions, I think I see, too. Picture a version of Benjamin's Angel of History that perhaps more closely approximates us: she's entirely encased in her anguish, and not looking at anything at all—what would there be to see? Behind her, there's a paradise she knows is now forever shut; before her, the world's new ruin.

Not that Pierce's jeering seventh-period slouches were trucking with Benjamin. Anything we grasped within Eve's face would have stemmed from our teacher's emphatic half-screech. She hollered, we shut up, and, eyes front, tried to look. Perhaps I'm inventing this, but I think I remember seeing something in Eve's face that, even then, seized me by my Izod collar and pummeled me into a different kind of silence. A silence that was ruptured by Ms. Price when she told us to notice the black streaks jutting out of Eden. "Those lines represent God's voice," she told us, "and He's pissed."

Even if our teacher here, yet again, traipsed away from facts, she yet again has a point: given long-standing cartoon convention, those choppy streaks look like a soundless bellowing or emanating spears of rage.

↶

One of many mistakes I've made here is reading the different shades of *The Expulsion*'s undercoat as segregating skies. In fact, those separate spheres in which the couple walks indicate the seams of Masaccio's *giornata*, pre-planned areas that fresco painters were able to finish in a single day. Because *buon fresco* involves applying paint directly onto a wall of wet plaster and allowing the pigment and plaster to fuse, artists had to work quickly on the designated fragment. Like the god of Genesis tackling his creation of the universe in piecemeal tasks, the fresco painter must determine in advance what might be reasonably completed before heading off to bed.

Examples of what was managed here in a single day include: The sky. The sky, the leafy branches and fruits of two trees. Part of the left hand, the fingers, with its corresponding background area. The sky and the angel. The upper part of the house. The tunic. The mantle. The mountains and the sky. The heads of the four standing figures. The four heads of the kneeling figures. The robes of the standing monk. The ground and part of the river. The small figures sitting in front of the house at the left. The woman with the baby in her arms. The body of the woman with her hand outstretched. The man with his back turned. The rest of the sky, the trees, and the urns. The wall with the window.

"Now thorns and thistles," God will say, "the earth shall bring forth for you." "Worth a look," Issa will write, "the thorny hedge, too, / in full bloom." And then, a few years after his daughter dies, seventeen syllables of joy: "Even the thorn bush / is blooming! / blooming!"

In *The Spring of My Life*, a memoir interweaving prose and haiku, Issa doesn't write extensively about the death of his children. His prose contextualization of his "world-of-dew" haiku (or should we call it his "and-yet" haiku?) lasts only about a page, and he doesn't mention his daughter by name. There, he describes the smallpox blisters on her body and tries out a few deathbed metaphors: water slipping under a bridge . . . blossoms scattered from a branch. But Issa, just then, is far from seeking consolation. A few lines before his faltering elegy, he writes in stark prose, "Her mother clutched her cold body and wailed."

And still, the chapter continues, spilling into an anthology of other poems written to commemorate dead children, slipping into a few Zen koans, and ending with a haiku that describes someone's goofball face hidden behind a multicolored fan. Which is just another form of trailing off, a lack of answers churning on and on.

Here's another story before these words fade, too.

On the orders of Theophilus, Peter has been imprisoned in Antioch and withers away in jail. Paul, disguised as a kind of odd-job handyman (yes, this is how the tale goes), convinces Theophilus to release the imprisoned saint on the condition that he resurrect the king's son, dead for fourteen years. "That," Peter deadpans, according to one translation of *The Golden Legend*, "is a hard promise to keep, Paul." But nonetheless the miracle takes place, and the boy's resurrection insists on its own "and-yet" fanfare.

Were Masaccio's Adam and Eve to keep walking in the direction they're headed, they'd tread across an even darker-colored earth that yields a view of mountaintop cottages and vineyards and a forever-rippling pale-jade lake. And although it wouldn't afford any consolation, maybe from that vantage point they could see the scene directly beneath them that depicts the raising of the son of Theophilus.

Masaccio's Theophilus panel is one of those jammed-packed fresco crowd scenes where patrons are honored, artist co-conspirators are included as a means of tipping one's hat (Brunelleschi), local characters are employed as wall-filler ("Hey, there's Lemmo the banker, with his crazy widow's peaks!"), and personages of antiquity collide with personages of contemporary life with no hesitations whatsoever. Not many of these folks, though, are bothering to look at the transpiring miracle. Some frown or seem bored or even suspicious: fair dues. I'm not buying it either—that this muscular lad, crouching on a circular cloth spread like a magician's hankie, was dead mere moments ago. Outside of the two skulls, the jawbone, the prop femurs scattered at his feet, there's not the faintest whiff of mortality in the scene.

Even Sloppy Tom, who's painted himself into this panel's far right edge, isn't looking anywhere near the center-stage hocus-pocus. And yet the artist rendered himself—out of reverence, convention, or because he wasn't sure what else his body should do—with one arm reaching toward the saint seated before him in a chair.

Or at least this is how it used to be, since a few years after Masaccio died (at the age of twenty-six, or twenty-seven, or twenty-eight—we're not quite sure), Filippino Lippi was hired to intervene. To finish what was left unfinished, add some additional scenes, and remove all traces of Sloppy Tom's arm extending toward the saint.

How easily the arm must have vanished. For Filippino, it didn't even amount to a day's work and left behind a small, nearly undetectable patch of what art historians term "confused color."

〜

What is gold—we know, we keep learning—doesn't last. And yet one of the few things that doesn't end is our need to circle back to what ends. To find ways of saying that nothing, not even this one beloved thing, can remain. To say, or nearly say, something in the wake of loss.

This, then, also isn't closure—how could it be?—and isn't intended to console. This is just me casting out a line—for caveats, a hand's breadth, a confusion of color, whatever might seem, at least for a while, to shoulder a bit of the day's work.

Looking out the window in this morning light, I can see, in the soon-to-be grass patch across the street, a glittering, light-winking wetness that will, given this scorching July, not last much longer. For now, though, dew blankets nearly everything I see—the mulch heaps, every needle on a newly planted spruce, those hardened squirts of dog shit on the curb, the little spear-tipped "Under Contract" sign I once watched some guy hammer into the lot's dirt, the thorny yucca where two ruby-throated hummingbirds beak-thrust each other from its shade. All this, too, answers nothing, I know, and yet I kept watching for a long while.

Monkey Mind

∽

A Meditative Path to Perfection

If my mind, at last, locks on a blank page, a cool patch of lake, perhaps a plain white wall, it might lead to an off-white hallway that leads to my childhood bedroom covered with that corny mural with its schools of pastel, lopsided clownfish and one rat-gray shark, frozen into place above the treasure chest's barely visible gold loot, a few feet below the mustard-yellow stenciled circle that was, of course, the sun. This wall painting was what my brother and I had wanted, yet when the woman asked, paintbrush in hand, still kneeling in her menthol cloud, "What do you think?"—what could we possibly have said? What should I have thought about our unchanging seascape, that crab now always not-scuttling toward the socket, the same frog-shaped cloud now forever stock-still?

I don't remember how long "forever" ended up being before, fickle kids, we had the scene whitewashed over. I do know that I saw our ocean's maker one last time. Sometimes, for dinner parties, my brother and I would be enlisted into lugging the guests' coats—heavy lengths of wool and fake fur that still gripped the night's cold—into the uncertain dark of my parents' room. We were encamped on the front stairs, killing time between new arrivals by playing War, halfheartedly flipping card after card (Queen takes the Eight, Four takes the Two, two Jacks means war), when she walked past with a glass of bourbon slush, scooped up the deck, riffled the cards in an expert blur, then read our minds, made Aces vanish, and plucked a Seven of Clubs from my brother's left ear.

Or I might narrow my mind to nothing but a field of breeze-rustled stems. Once, while playing Funny Face, a children's board game where players mime actions written on cards (*Brush your teeth. Make a snowman. Pull someone from a deep hole.*), my wife read the next instructions to our son—*Be grass blowing in the wind*—and, without a second's pause, he rocked on his feet from side to side, grinning, sure we'd guess what he meant. What the grasses mean I'm not at all sure, but I do know when someone once asked Brahms late in his life about the secret to composing music, the cigar-musty Maestro, without missing a beat, replied, "Take more walks in the woods." Which I might do, even today, watching for camp-robber jays and scuttling lizards. I might feel our pine-scattered earth giving back the sun's heat, and no doubt wedge my nose into the bark niche of a ponderosa and sniff that vanilla smell.

In the summer before leaving for college, I worked in the produce department of a grocery store, where, among other things, I packaged fruit and vegetables on flimsy Styrofoam trays: white cherries and watermelon slices, trimmed rhubarb and testicular figs, confetti-shredded cabbage, rosemary spears, clam-shaped halves of radicchio. For hours, I might do nothing more than gather grapes from wax-coated boxes, center them on the tray, swaddle the still-wet bunches in plastic wrap, and for a two-second beat ("not one, not three") press the package to a heated pad which would melt the plastic and seal the item shut. Some days, among the soggy crates of stale walnuts, kale, corn on the cob, and pears, I'd be entirely alone with my singular task. Other times, I'd make my little parcels of things while yabbering with Steve about baseball, or arguing with Kristie about abortion, or listening to Big Jim, who didn't talk much but sang, inevitably, nearly every shift, misremembered lines of "Is You Is or Is You Ain't My Baby." Pluck, center, swaddle; press, wait, melt. Pluck, center—"Maybe that baby's found someone new." Swaddle, drop—"Or could my baby still be my baby true?"—wait, melt.

Or I could picture, I'm told, as a means of emptying the mind, any task performed again and again. Bundling my paper route's stacks of finger-blackening *Hudson Hubs*, squeegeeing goose shit from Dover Lake's tangle of sidewalks. And then I'm hunched, almost kneeling, moving across Blossom Music Center's outdoor amphitheater. Each morning following a concert, our job in Maintenance is to walk slowly up the hill, then slowly back down, bagging the detritus left behind. We must not use gloves, we must not veer from our imagined rows, we must keep our eyes on the grass at all times. Corks, gum, chicken bones, condoms; bottle caps, roach clips, lollipop sticks, coins, the collar of a dog named Tic-Tac.

Whatever was found could be kept, although admittedly my own rewards were slim—once, a rugby shirt (post–New Kids on the Block); once, some damp pizza still in the box (post–Huey Lewis and the News) that served as a perfect midmorning snack for our sun-scorched crew. The year before, we'd been told, someone found a hundred-dollar bill; the year before that (post-Motörhead, behind Bathroom 6), someone found the stabbed body of a biker.

I can't say I'm ever looking for absence. I've never understood why mindfulness couldn't be constituted by a brimming-full mind. I might begin with field-scruff scrunched up where coyotes bedded down, or a sad light streaking one of Hopper's rooms—then, who knows? I might begin with the empty nuthatch nest wedged into the back of a newspaper box, but soon enough, magpie-like, I'm grappling after the dented, moonlight-grazed hood of that five a.m. Camaro from which the newspaper is pitched onto the drive.

So much empty dugout bench surrounds a pitcher on the cusp of flinging a perfect game. Abiding baseball superstition, perhaps knowing that humans shouldn't mingle with saints, his teammates won't speak to him, won't make eye contact. Even the game's announcers avoid saying anything that might connote perfection, relying instead on silent camera shots of the scoreboard's rows of zeros. During ads for lobster legs and lite beer, fans watching from home know better than to acknowledge the events at hand. Otherwise, who knows what our decidedly imperfect words might make transpire—strike zone shrinkage, a cleanup's blooper into left, or something even more unspeakable.

May 15, 1981. Len Barker, the Big Donkey, who once fired a ball from the mound straight into Fenway's press box (now lauded as the wildest pitch ever thrown), was hauling through the Blue Jays' lineup in a forty-nine-degree Cleveland drizzle. He's laying off the changeup, tucking into his fastball and an out-of-nowhere curve with a stellar red-herring delivery. Who knows when Barker caught a whiff of what could be in the offing, but game footage of the top of the seventh shows a fan, in anticipation of flawlessness, wearing an enormous foam sombrero, gyrating unhinged in the box seats.

By the ninth, that unspoken word lumbers in the air, and Barker is suddenly sweating it. He's so close that he can't grip the ball as he walks from the dugout, and once he even stumbles off the mound. And then, with a third base pop-up to Harrah, a struck-out-swinging fastball, and Ernie Whitt, reaching for an outside corner, chopping a ball to Manning in center who caught it in a few quick strides, there it was: perfection.

Two weeks later, against all odds, perfection was slow-brewing yet again in the Mistake-on-the-Lake. We were driving to the Sandusky docks and, to pass the time while scrunched up in the backseat with my brother and sister (because this is what I sometimes did), I'm staring out the window, imagining that our car is plunging deep into the dirt only to rise a few yards later, airborne, before plunging into earth again. We were either plunging or soaring or plunging again—as if our car were some enormous needle stitching earth to sky—when I heard my father shatter the cardinal Perfect Game rule. "Oh my god, he's doing it," my dad blurts. "He's doing it again." It should have been verboten, lugging out those words just then, except that, unbelievably, the Big Donkey seemed to be hacking out yet another path to transcendence. He was towering again on a rain-soaked mound, and no one had yet reached first. It's only after Harrah makes the exact same crowd-diving, nearly heels-over-ass catch that something dawns on my dad: how could it be raining in Cleveland? There's barely a cloud in sight and we're cruising past sun-gleaming silos. The only reason that pant-hitching Len Barker would be perfect yet again was that, unbeknownst to us, we were listening to a rebroadcast of the earlier game. Perfecto verbatim. Who knew?

I used to strike out in T-ball. Sometimes, when staying as a guest, I'll piss in a friend's shower. I can't seem to learn how to make a fly fishing Nail Knot, or a Clinch Knot, or a Perfection Loop, which means I'll never watch, fly rod in hand, a rainbow trout tail-twitching between my waders. This list, of course, could go on and on, but such things are not quite what I mean. What I mean is that, for many years, I thought what turned and lifted us from the earth was not called the Ferris Wheel (named after its inventor, George Washington Gale Ferris Jr.) but the Fairest Wheel—as in the fairest wheel of all.

Hiroshi Sugimoto, just after a project focused on natural-history dioramas (five gemsbok peering from a constructed savanna; our hairy distant relatives, strolling arm in arm, leaving footprints in volcanic ash), but before he photographed wax effigies at Madame

Tussauds' (Arafat, Anne Boleyn, Judas, Princess Di) and seascapes, electromagnetic charges, Kyoto's 1,001 armed and merciful Bodhisatt- vas, and then a single breeze-flickering flame, set up his camera in the rear of a movie theater and timed his exposure to last the exact length of the film being screened.

Inspired for this project by "a near hallucinatory vision," Sugimoto heard a voice asking, "Suppose you shoot a whole movie in a single frame?" The answer, unwavering, emphatic: "You get a shining screen." Which is partially true: all these photos wield a dead-center, whiter-than-white rectangle, the film having been trans- formed into a haunting, Rothko-like blare of light.

But, without apologies, I doubt I'd spend much time looking at shining square after square were it not for whatever else was snared in each movie-house glow. On the outskirts of each tidy frame of luminescence, there's a nearly inexhaustible array of things. Chande- liers, exit signs, scaffolds, cables, curtains, furled-up flags. There are rows of pipes meant to resemble the setting sun, murals of Grecian urns. There are mostly empty, pew-like seats, and some seats where audience members ghost, blurred by the long exposure, seeming to vibrate as if in the throes of rapture. In the shot of the Akron Civic Theater—a palatial, hallowed spot where I once doffed my foam antlers as the Bullwinkle festival began—I can see parapets, the Alhambra-style arch, lavish egg-and-dart ornaments, Corinthian columns, and alabaster cupids with bows and arrows; what I can't see, but know is hidden within the photograph's top third of sheer black, is that theater's gilded faux-night sky, with its translucent, motorized clouds and electric-bulb constellations.

If, as Sugimoto has claimed, the emanating light varies in slight gradations depending on the kind of movie being shown (a film noir, say, versus a chummy comedy), I can't detect such subtleties myself.

On the one hand, here is a distilled and rarified essence, a revelation of what we've been looking at all along. "Those with a feeling for refinement," Bashō wrote, "find joy in knowing the truth and insight of things." And yet, no matter what these photographs might suggest about time and shadow and revelation, these photographs sanitize, via that unvarying light, what all of us—those vibrating, butter-smutched schlubs—hope to lose ourselves in, what we've gathered unsaintly for: neck-pinching Vulcans or Dachau slums or an unfazed, pun-cracking cartoon moose cascading down the side of a cliff.

The word for meditate in Hebrew is *hagah*, which means not only "to ponder" but also, in an unpredictable litany of verbs, to groan, sigh, murmur in pleasure, murmur in anger, to utter, to roar. You may begin a journey in reverential silence, as Thoreau once did, sauntering through Hubbard's Grove. But after he glimpsed the first woodchuck of the season, he bolted after him, cutting him off against the fence and squatting close by. He began by studying its two-inch whiskers, then taunted it with a stick, then stared into its chestnut eyes, unmoving, for half an hour, just before he offered it some chewed-up checkerberry leaves and spoke—cooing, burbling, babbling, sighing—in "quasi forest lingo." "My needle is slow to settle," he wrote.

Which was also true for Diane Arbus, who—where did I hear this?—began her career by taking photographs of a single lightbulb dangling in a closet. "A photograph is a secret about a secret," she once said, and perhaps she was seeking the essence of light or the riddles of line afforded by a glimpse of filament. We'll never know how long it was before this single-bulb project happily ran her smack-dab into a wall, but soon enough she was hoofing it down fire escapes, wandering Hell's Kitchen dives. She was lingering at strip shows, ballrooms, nudist camps, Coney Island Freak Show tents, the cross-dresser's musty bedroom. *A Jewish Giant at Home with His Parents in the Bronx, N.Y., 1970; Child with Toy Hand Grenade in Central Park, N.Y.C.,* 1962—even her titles usher us through tiny veering journeys.

"My favorite thing is to go where I've never been," Arbus wrote. "Who but the Evil One has cried 'Whoa!' to mankind?" Thoreau asked. Unapologetically, then, *A* might be followed by *H,* which might be followed by twelve or mauve, before bounding off who knows where. It's grappling after vine, then beetle or berry, then whatever's glimmering in grass-rot, or even grass-rot itself. It might be the wholehearted bushwhack to a spot that seemed, just a moment before, hidden from sight—perhaps a place of distilled luminescence, perhaps where the floors are forever-sticky with Dr. Pepper and Jujubes and Charles Bronson fills the horizon, grinning, as he makes his hand into an L-shaped gun.

It's a day when I had nothing particular planned but found it cluttered with bills, drafts of a sonnet doomed to fail, then a few breathy tenor tracks of Eddie Harris while forking avocado onto torn chunks of rosemary bread. I half-watched most of *Serpico*—no hike, after all—before heading to Padres for two cold Lone Stars and then, on impulse, joined a tipsy caravan to the Mystery Lights' viewing station, a place where we all stood and watched some distant specks of light that some claim we'll never understand, some claim are headlights skating Highway 67.

Either way, lights appeared, vanished, reappeared, and seemed to wander through air, and we lost track of the night and the scattershot bursts of pumpkin-orange lightning behind us. Someone said, "It's like a set of eyes," and someone said, "I've never seen one that high before," followed by "Kendra, get your heinie over here." Then someone said, "That one was perfect," and, in unison—who knew?—we all agreed that it was.

Against Desire

⌐⌐

Years ago, I shared a house with a greenhorn Buddhist in the suburbs of Boston. All through the summer heat, I watched him bow and kneel before an upturned VCR box on which he had perched his smirking, pot-bellied, four-inch plastic figurine. Out on the front porch, page-skimming toward my August goal of finishing *Ulysses*, I could smell his sandalwood resin and, through the blinds, glimpse his movements that, at least to my knee-jerk adolescent mind, resembled genuflecting.

I knew little about his chosen spiritual path, but I did know that his self-proclaimed quest to purge himself of desire began with a $10.99 mass-manufactured Buddha propped on a box that was itself a newly emptied vessel for a vessel of desires. And I knew he had once scampered off to the library in order to seek out loopholes in his chosen doctrine that would allow him, conscience cleared, to lure a flirty cashier to his sheets.

To my mind, Molly Bloom's rhapsodic, pure-gravy *Yes*—perhaps all I understood of Joyce then—served as the incontrovertible answer to his abstentions.

⌐⌐

Thus I don't mean the shedding of it, its deferral or transcendence. I'm thinking only of the word. Because of late it's been employed as a crutch, a fill-in, a tic. A workhorse brushing shoulders with universal truth wherever it might amble. *Desire*—enjambed, spotlighted, left dangling on the page, intended to shoulder the weight of all that we might want.

Desire, from the Latin, coupling *de*—down, off, away—and *sidus*—constellations, heavenly bodies. Yet where within these composite roots is our wet-mouth pining? Our nagging need to touch, seize, lick, knee a crotch, dodge, feed? Where is longing's shell game, palimpsest, or fuse, our hands grappling after detergent, the soup spoon, a thigh? Where is craning one's neck to find the hordes of swallows you saw, just the other day, at this exact spot, flitting between the cars while waiting for the light to turn green?

Desire, in its insistence on distance and the stuff of the stars, protests too much. Even its etymology is a lie.

↬

I once traveled across the sea to be with a woman I thought I loved. In a resort town in the south of England, I rented a cramped bed-sit above a massage parlor masquerading as a disco that, on several occasions that summer, was raided by police who seemed content, as far as I could tell from my window perch, to laugh it off in return for handjobs or cash bribes. I lied my way into a job at Old Orleans, an American-themed bar, where I wore a gold fleur-de-lis vest and botched cocktails with names like Sex on the Beach and Between the Sheets and learned to spin bottles on my palm.

Within weeks, I'd peeked into the depths of my girlfriend's journal, learned about a long stream of infidelities I won't rehash here, and packed her books and clothes into a drawstring laundry bag that I dumped—dramatically, self-consciously—at her feet on a beach of stones. Saddled with a lease, I continued to serve watered-down drinks, including glass after glass of double-rum Hurricanes to a man who began appearing at the bar almost daily, bringing me, once, a canary-yellow anthology of American poets and, once, an offer to pay to watch me dance. After quitting my job, I traveled to Paris, where, suddenly happier than I had ever been, I killed evenings in a fork-less, plate-less, one-room apartment, plucking sauce-less spaghetti off newspapers spread across my lap.

Tell me, even within this small window of longings (a tame one, reader, that I'm willing to share), what is the one umbrella term?

Choose any two things at all—banjo lessons, a biopsy report, the cable guy now more than three hours late, a fistful of unsalted cashews, the man who hammers a roadside cross into the dirt and will never stop wishing his daughter alive—then tell me all wanting is the same.

～

This morning, frothing milk for my coffee, while nagging my young son who had stalled with only one leg in his patched-up corduroys, I heard on NPR one of those lighthearted interludes they love to unfurl before the real business of the day (i.e., a woman gives birth to twins on her birthday, after which the presiding doctor announces it's his birthday as well, followed by the news from Haiti, the unemployment index, a championship, yet another marketplace bomb). In less than fifteen seconds, I learned that an eleven-year-old boy, after winning an essay competition, was allowed to implode Texas Stadium.

Ah, desire, I'd thought at first, as if those two protracted syllables sufficiently exhausted the tale. As if one word could uniformly blanket everyone among the thousands who gathered, fists clenched, hooting into sky, taking pre-dawn snapshots that lit the stadium's parking lot in bright, fleeting bursts.

Casey Rogers earned the opportunity to destroy this landmark not by writing about his love of rubbernecking ruin (as I'd hoped and guessed), but rather collecting cans of beans and toothpaste for the Dallas homeless. Wearing a prop hardhat, he turned a switch, then turned his head to watch the stadium disappear in a curtain of dust. One of the broadcasters called it "a masterpiece"; one mentioned the building had been designed with a hole in its roof "so that God could watch His team." The Kraft Corporation, sponsors of the event, proclaimed in a press release, "We think our new Cheddar Explosion is dynamite." On YouTube, I watched Casey's father and an ex-cheerleader weep.

Forget any one word—I mean something else entirely. Something sticky with sweat, buzzed on green-apple wine coolers, crouched at a knothole in the waterslide park's changing room, aching for one lousy nipple. Something with lint-crammed pockets, instant pudding in the fridge, a mallet, a Tuesday follow-up at the orthodontist. Something chewing a jelly donut while a stadium implodes and parking lot asphalt trembles.

I mean a thirst that rises, unbidden, driving me to sit here, listening to a squabble of jays and a weedwhacker's drone while staring at the monitor's pulsing cursor, unsure, if not *desire*, what word I should type.

"You'll have to tell me all about it," I've found myself saying to my son as he heads off somewhere—a movie, a playdate, a park, or school—he's gagging to go.

"But I can't tell you *all* about it," he reminds me again.

One Hundred Twenty-One Seconds of Square Dance among Other Things

Some dingbat, never-seen-him-before kid wearing an aviator cap blinks and smirks at the camera. Cut to my mother—four, maybe five—waving in spastic flaps, fiddling with a doll, exhaling plumes of breath. She sits on a pink stool in the center of a lawn, then someone's coat sleeve blocks the lens, then she grips the steering wheel of a ride-on toy car and—it's hard not to read this as a gesture that cues—begins to turn it, arm over arm.

A burst of dark, a swarm of blue-yellow specks, and then we're deep within some indiscernible world and all the dead are dancing.

From the looks of it, they've been at it for hours and we join them midstride, midspin, midlaugh. They twirl, pivot, body-buck, gallop—this is no ballroom glide—gallivant, tumble from view. A whirl of plaid, of a lime-green blouse, of locked arms in a blur.

A dance, darkness, the dead. I know this alliterative procession may sound thunderous, and it's maybe worth saying from the outset that all I'm watching is poorly lit footage of my grandparents' friends romp-stomping through a square dance many decades back. Against a wall of dark forged by poor lighting—I don't mean to diminish so much as describe—one can literally see nothing but bodies rotating through black space. Stripped of all grounding details—a table with a punch bowl, for instance, or a glimpse of a framed painting that might clearly announce *the church basement over on Monroe*—it's as if these figures threaded the boundless ether. Or is that too thunderous, too?

The moment—or rather this stop-start assemblage of shots— lasts one second beyond the two-minute mark, and is crammed into what is now a movie-length DVD that houses my grandmother's 8mm films (discovered, after she died, stashed in an oversized Tupperware beneath her bed). No matter what you might think of wading through decade-spanning home movies, let alone a gaggle of anonymous hoedowning Toledoans, here, if nothing else, is two minutes of insulated, hurly-burly joy. Not to mention grace, since even within the scrambled mishmash of partners, the false spins and misplaced steps, there's a suppleness to how these bodies move. To how hands reach out and, somehow, always, the hand of someone else reaches in turn, unwavering response to each and every call.

The light from the camera must be blinding, although no one seems to mind. In fact, no one seems to notice revolving into this narrow flare of light at all, so completely do they give themselves over to their task. Which is to do-si-do and mean it—every lurch, bow, crossover, promenade. Flutter Wheel, Scoot Back, Cloverleaf. Split the Outside. Pass the Ocean. Except rather than intricate, orchestrated steps—Ping-Pong Circulate? Teacup Chain?—everyone here seems to just scoot and Ping-Pong carefree. Then two minutes later, the scene is done, and all the dancers gone.

But back up, rewind, scroll back. Before this disc lurches breakneck ahead toward shots of my grandmother chucking snowballs at the camera and a half-dozen Boy Scouts scrubbing barrels—who knows why?—and my mother wielding a toy machine gun and someone bowing in a doorway, commemorating something, I want to linger at this hoedown (words, admittedly, I never thought I'd say). I can't seem to let these two minutes go.

Take, for instance, even this video's silence. At first, I resented the disorienting soundlessness of these shots, which is not to say I wanted to hear fiddles and foot-stomp and a caller's nasal commands. It's only that, upon my first viewing, I craved the white-noise whirr of a projector's motor and the muted rattle of spinning reels that for me have come to signal, Pavlov-like, travels through the long-gone past.

Beginning his journey to the Underworld, Ulysses follows the north wind's breath to a grove of poplars and the rock where two roaring rivers merge before digging a two-foot trench and pouring libations of honeyed milk, then wine, then water with a pinch of barley. Aeneas, in order to commune with his father's shade, must slaughter a herd of wine-drenched cows, construct a pyre of cypress, oak, and berry-wielding rowan, and then find and pluck a parasitical golden bough that grows deep in the forest and is, by all accounts, impossible to both find and pluck. And before these particular visions of the past were transferred via the magic of U-Betcha Video to this palm-sized glimmering disc, I would always, and in this order, position a white sheet over the fireplace, heave the instruction-less, eBay-auctioned projector from its case, angle it on a table, adjust the tilt knob, lift the rear wheel, lock the desired reel in place, thread the film's end over the sprockets and through a labyrinth of curves and slots, flip the direction lever to forward, turn the control switch to motor, engage the rear wheel, turn the control switch to lamp, and, maintaining vigilance, keeping one hand poised should the film begin to burn from the projector's unforgiving heat, only then earn the right to commune for a few minutes with the dead.

Versus now. Now, I slide in a disc, touch play, and—voilà!—all the cued-up shades swim back.

Gradually, though, I've come to terms with the ease of this new format. For one thing, there's the lure of this disc's hodge-podge scramble of footage now that all the old individual reels are spliced together as one. After all, the mind doesn't sustain an orderly focus on, for example, that trip to Jamaica with its nibbled sugarcane and farmer-tanned chicken fights in the pool before, available images exhausted, sidestepping to a peculiar vision of your great-grandmother raising a teakettle with great earnestness on the sidewalk, signaling something you'll never understand. Far closer to how memory works is this madcap scurrying that's been loosed from cause and effect: a wind-up poodle, a waterfall, pop flies, a pony; a garden, more Boy Scouts doing something with barrels, a clump of perch strung through the gills and held out like some impossible blossom.

And then there's the church-like silence that, in lieu of the projec-tor's whir and the depleted reel's rhythmic tail-end flap, has become the exclusive soundtrack of these shots. If nothing else, the sound-lessness of the scene underscores a conceit I can't resist: it's as if I've been afforded a peephole glimpse of Heaven, a vision of the Hereafter that, for once, I can abide. For one beat past two minutes—arguably all of infinity we could possibly understand—the jazzed-up dead stomp and reel, clasp hands, and fling themselves about. There's no Dantesque thrashing whirlwind, and there's no puppeteer caller bellowing "Shoot the Star" or "Cast a Shadow" or other phrases dictating how the body must move. Here, the dead happily wing it, careening on their own tipsy volition.

The ease of all this allowed me to watch the film even more, which made me notice the lousy lighting that began to seem beauti-ful, which made me want to watch it all yet again. Which is when I noticed my own grandfather whirling past.

There he is—nearly unrecognizable in his unfettered youth, beaming, bangs flopping in his face—and then he's gone, wheeling out of sight, replaced by someone I've never seen before. There he is again, in the background this time, barely visible and knowable only by his now-knowable plaid shirt. Then he's gone just before surging into the foreground again, exuberant, the barest sheen of sweat on his forehead.

He's working hard, even in his joy. He always worked hard: barges, boilers, hoists, hulls, turbines, condensers, ash pits, and other words I wish that I could claim I learned from him, rather than trotting out a few things that comprised his life, stringing them up here without context.

He worked until something wadded his heart into a fist and, upon being ordered to work less, still found ways to work. There was still a need for a bit of welding down at the Maumee docks, and—screwdriver in hand, always midtask—there was squirrel-proofing the birdfeeder, tightening a dribbling nozzle, wiring the miniature porch lights and chandeliers of another custom dollhouse, hammering together the hinged lockbox he must have known I'd use to stash my recess-bartered porn. Clutching a mallet, gumming a nail, right up until Alzheimer's stopped him, he was unstoppable.

Although even now that I've recognized him, giddy and sauntering through steps he doesn't know, it'd be disingenuous to suggest that, each time I watch this film, I'm honing in on his work ethic and calloused hands. Sometimes, instead, I love the way these bodies become, inevitably, nothing but body distilled to an essence, removed from any individual life: anonymous hands grapple for hands, shapes of flesh spill into view, and there are glimpses of bright-lit flittering selves before each tumbles into darkness again.

Pause the shot anywhere, and, with astonishing clarity, a hand or

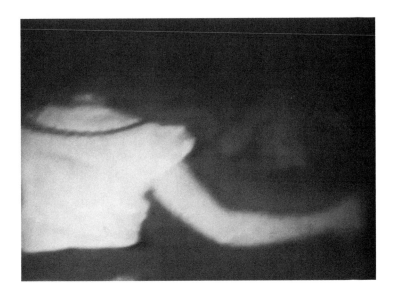

chest or flailing sleeve ghosts in a pool of black like some cropped Caravaggio detail. And even if it might seem misplaced here to trot out a word like *chiaroscuro,* how else to describe the effect of that light or its lack? Or, more to the point of my own prescribed movements, I doubt I could convey that stark collision between darkness and light without, out of habit or simply as a crutch, hauling out an artist for reference. We see Turner sunsets, O'Keeffe stargazers in a vase, a procession of Van Gogh cypress, and, sometimes, if we're lucky, Caravaggian deep wells of black.

These Toledo square dancers may not much resemble the figures from Caravaggio's *Supper at Emmaus*—perhaps that goes without saying?—although when I freeze-frame this footage of the dance, I can't help but see a correspondence. In the story—you know this—two disciples meet a man on the road three days after the Crucifixion; they invite him to dinner, sit down to eat, and only then realize that their companion is Jesus, who promptly disappears. In Caravaggio's painting, one of the disciples begins to rise in burgeoning delight, the other flings open his arms, yet this fleeting blessing takes place against a wall's backdrop of brown that dissolves into shadowy murk.

Which is not to say there's nothing else to look at. Caravaggio gives us the tablecloth's too-white sheen, shimmering glasses of water and wine, light flecking the rim of the shriveled date that has tumbled from the main-course roasted bird, and that basket of fruit which hangs impossibly over the table's edge, as if anticipating the miracle to come with a little aperitif razzle-dazzle. Nonetheless, darkness encases the scene, and there's little to orient the viewer.

Titian, rendering this same meal, provides a backdrop of mountains, gilded clouds, a distant sun-barraged tree. Even Van Meegeren the forger, scheming his way toward Emmaus and a Vermeer-slanted light, counters his backdrop's blackness with a window that hums with a faux seventeenth-century gleam he layered in with a badger-hair brush. Caravaggio seems to be suggesting that such things merely distract from the undeserved plentitude at hand. Or at least this is how I take it. We have, after all, the sufficient splendor of a meal, a single recognition, a reaching-after before someone is inexplicably gone.

Footage of the square dance stops, dissolves again into specks, and cuts to a house where guests are arriving. There's a dinner party beginning: hats are doffed, coats shrugged loose, and everyone smiles wide-mouth as they're caught strolling through the door. At first, this shot, too, seems disconnected from what preceded it, another free-floating moment on the past's wide sea. And then there's the same plaid shirt, the same lime-green blouse, as bright and memorable as the crimson top Jesus wears in Caravaggio's painting.

This is, I realized, the post-dance portion of the same night, and our world—complete with striped drapes, a spackled doorway, some hideous couch—has now been restored. Everyone blinks hard, as if not having anticipated this late-night meal, as if just awakened from the long wash of a dream.

And there's my grandfather, suddenly, yet again. Just now, utterly content, he doesn't look at all like someone's grandfather, but just a man named Hank who's nicknamed Mabel for reasons he hauled to his grave. He's biting into a wedge of bratwurst, now a paprika-dusted deviled egg. He's earned it. He's always earned it. His feet ache, and in silence he sips a lukewarm beer, which, of course, he's earned, too, by working all night through yet more verbs he proved he could handle just fine. Wheel and Deal, Box the Gnat. Walk and Dodge, Explode the Wave.

And then he's gone.

No Fuller on Earth

〜

In Raphael's *Transfiguration*, above the bunched-up folds of monochrome robes, above all those gesticulating hands, above Mount Tabor rising up like a little dough-dented knoll just a few feet above the earth, a man has become light and hovers midair and—this is not how we know it to be—remains light forevermore.

〜

Here is the story in brief: not long after ascending the mountain with three of his disciples, Jesus became like the sun. It was, scripture tells us, as if his very flesh turned to light. The spirits of Moses and Elijah appeared, and Peter pledged to build three tabernacles for prayer, and a cloud wafted forth, demanding we pay heed, and the disciples pitched forward in fear, transfixed.

Yet, as always, the light didn't last, and soon enough they were all threading down the mountain's switchbacking trail. Soon enough, too, they encountered a man within a crowd who begged Jesus to cure his ailing son, and then the talk turned from all that impossible light to the path of mortal flesh.

〜

In one photograph—perhaps this was just before she was diag-
nosed?—Kate stands in the doorway of her studio. It's one of those
dazzling, sun-soaked New Mexico winter days, and behind her the
sky is a searing, cloudless swatch of blue. Dressed in a black shirt,
black jeans, and a nearly fluorescent fuchsia down vest, she's flashing
one of her beaming, all-in smiles even as she squints in the glare.
Although she's leaning against the door's frame, one leg is angled
forward, as if she were already in the act of stepping away from this
snapshot's pause, already pivoting back into her studio where she'll
begin once again stacking, cutting, aligning, sewing, making some
soon-to-be-beautiful new thing.

↜

Some quibble that the Transfiguration's light falls short of the crite-
ria for a miracle. Apparently mere radiance is not enough, especially
when compared to Lazarus beginning to breathe once again or that
water darkening into wine. Moreover, it's been said that the moment
of brilliance and change just didn't last long enough.

For others, though, that brevity, that temporary suspension of the
natural order, is one of the defining characteristics of the miraculous.
How long, after all, could the blindsiding last before it became simply the way things run?

↜

In one of Kate's sculptures, white cloth has been coiled into a small
wooden frame. It's a compact piece—just a foot long, perhaps six
inches high—and the fabric seems to both resist and embrace its
box-like constraints: the cloth curves in crimped little waves, then
doubles back on itself in dramatic whorls. It reminds me of stretched
taffy or a Van Gogh sky, of batter poured into a pan, of intestines or
thumbprint swirls.

↜

A quick Google search sends me to *Wikipedia*, which links me to chapter 9 of the Gospel according to Mark, where this time I'm confounded less by the Transfiguration's narrative (yes, even that talking cloud and the spirit of Moses paddling air) than simply the scripture's matter-of-fact tone. While the moment would seem to lend itself to a speechless awe, the Bible's description strides through similes at a quick clip, as if cocksure each word will get it right.

Thus we're told a man became as luminous as the sun. His robes, caked with trail dust just a moment before, turned white as snow. *Exceedingly so*, the scriptures insist. His robes—behold—in fact became whiter than any fuller on earth might bleach them.

‿

Because the painting has become so familiar (its showcase status in the Vatican Museum; the painting's own nine-year transfiguration into a eighteenth-century mosaic installed in Saint Peter's Basilica), it's easy to overlook how seriously strange Raphael's *Transfiguration* is. Look again at its clutter of color, that confusion of hands, the baffling conflation of time and space. Although the transformation itself occurs on the mountain peak, and although in the Bible the crowd greets Jesus only after he's tramped back down Mount Tabor, the two moments in the painting seem to be taking place at the same time, so that foreground and background, miracle and aftermath, fleeting light and convulsing boy are unfolding all at once.

Some in the crowd point at the man hovering in the light, some point at the flailing child. Some shield their eyes or clutch their chest, overwhelmed by it all.

〜

Minimalist art doesn't always speak to me, and, depending on which varnished cube or fluorescent light cluster I'm looking at, I can find myself feeling twitchy while trying to contend with the stubborn reticence of some rarefied object.

With Kate's spare and haunting work, however, I've consistently experienced a kind of quiet rapture, most especially with her sculpture entitled *Through*. The piece could hardly be simpler in its composition: thin strips of Baltic birch plywood are compressed together to form a mounted board about three feet long, and a small length of gray wool felt, positioned behind the wood, has been slit in two places so that the board slips through it.

The first time I saw it, I found myself transfixed by its collision of shape, texture, and form. The wood's accruing striations stand out against the felt's uniform gray, and the fabric's soft fin-like shapes droop in contrast to the wood's unwavering, ruler-straight lines. It would be a corny contrivance, of course, to endow this piece with a voice, and yet to my mind this sculpture has always seemed to quietly insist that its own unlikely, uneasy harmony is the only harmony on earth to be had.

〜

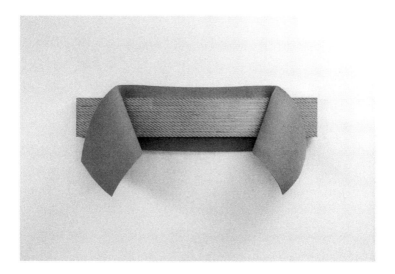

As you stand beneath the gridded domed glass ceiling of the Vatican Museum's room number eight, gazing up at *The Transfiguration* from behind the roped-off barrier, the painted light that surrounds Jesus looks radiantly white. Whiter, yes, than any bleached robes imaginable, whiter than the snow hurling down outside my window just now. It seems whiter than a heap of sugar or a globby Wite-Out smear—for how else but through the lens of the earthly can we ever understand the divine?—or even Marilyn's dress above the subway vent gusting around her thighs.

All these comparisons fail, of course, but for reasons beyond my own ill-chosen words. When I page through a book of close-up reproductions of the painting, it's clear that Raphael's light is made not merely of a glistering white. Rather, it's speckled with age, and bristle-streaked, and composed of hints of blue and what looks like a mustardy ochre.

"I choose to cut my materials by hand, when possible, so that within this fairly mundane stacking process there is room for the unexpected," Kate has written about her work. "The inescapable imperfection of something cut by hand (or drawn by hand) has its own irregular, flawed beauty that gives the work a human quality I find necessary and inevitable."

❧

There are two things I remember vividly about the funeral of a high school friend who died from a brain tumor many years back. One was the shock of seeing her embalmed body in the open casket, how her distorted face seemed like some amateur sketch of the woman I had known and adored. The other was walking out the parlor's back door and, on impulse, striding over to an evergreen at the edge of the parking lot, yanking off a fistful of needles, and breathing in the scent of pine.

Here, it seems to me, is one possible paradox of loss. At times, those proximities to death, those sudden intimations of mortality, seem to heighten our awareness of the world that surrounds us. Then again, grappling after that same "now-ness" can also lure us away from the person we're grieving for. Pine scent gives way to a cardinal's scarlet flare, followed by wind-twitching ditch grass or the precise hook-shaped back end of an otherwise bulbous cloud and countless other minute scraps from the world of ten thousand things.

No matter the spirit of that turning away, it's a departure nonetheless, one as clear-cut as the moment Auden traces in his poem about Brueghel's painting of Icarus. There, a winged boy plummets from the sky, and while many don't notice his descent at all—the ploughman continues to guide his blade through earth, dogs stutter on with their little doggy lives—the passengers aboard a ship witness what takes place. They see something amazing, and yet the sea is still rippling in the spot where the boy disappeared before those on board remember they have somewhere else to be, and calmly sail on.

∽

Some early critics felt that *The Transfiguration* ignored basic artistic principles of harmony and coherence: the mind must parse and cleave the narratives (one about light, one about human frailty) at the same time that, we're expected to understand, the two parts need to be addressed as inseparable pieces of the same story. It's as if Raphael has created a kind of cinematic split-screen without bothering to split the screen.

Goethe, on the other hand, far from being disturbed by Raphael's contortions of space, felt that the painting's two halves needed each other, like a yin solemnly spooning a yang. Through adjacency and simultaneity, a dialogue between agony and transcendence is forged. Besides, should you require the verisimilitude of a horizon, Raphael has provided that too: there it is, crammed into a center-right sliver of the canvas, set off into the deep distance, miles behind the darkened branches of some shaggy-leafed tree. Back within that blue haze, there's also a glimpse of city walls, nearly indistinguishable from the shrubby hillside, and perhaps serving as a reminder of all the bruised bodies and unhealed flesh that Christ, after becoming pure light, will neither encounter nor cure during his mountain descent.

About suffering, they were never wrong, the Old Masters.

∽

Although given what X-rays and drafts of Raphael's painting reveal, he was apparently wrong many times. At one point, those awe-struck apostles who shield their eyes on Mount Tabor's summit were going to be rendered entirely nude. At one point, rather than painting him floating midair, no longer quite of our element, Raphael was going to depict Christ gleaming bright but with his feet perched on a lumpy boulder.

Perhaps I should clarify: Raphael's struggle with the painting's composition didn't take place within the darkened lower half where the crowd gathers around the wild-eyed boy. Instead, all his reworking and uncertainty took place in the realm of light.

↬

At first, we knew only what Kate had chosen to announce to friends: the cancer had spread through her body and no one was sure if the chemotherapy would work. In the feeblest of gestures, and since there was no clear sense of what else to do, my wife and I made a pot of minestrone soup that I drove across town and left on her doorstep. For a long time, I sat behind the wheel of the car, staring at the light that fell indiscriminately on her house, the sidewalk, the parked cars and trees, the shattered glass at the bus stop, the charred yellow sun of the Burrito Spot's sign down the block. That light which is everywhere, and promises nothing, and forces us to guess what it means.

↬

Home, a piece that Kate installed in a gallery in Vermont, is a semi-translucent tent-shaped structure made of sailcloth. Its design is simple, as if a child's drawing of a house were somehow inflated and left to hang balloon-like from the ceiling where it dangles aglow, seemingly weightless, illuminated by two lights inside.

Despite its title, however, and despite its beacon-like gleam, I can only see the place that the piece depicts as inhospitable. It hovers not far from the gallery floor, lovely to look upon and seemingly welcoming with its warm light; at the same time—and perhaps like any vision of heaven—it remains out of reach, unable to support any real human weight, sealed shut with long seams of dark stitches.

↬

In order to depict that holy light, Raphael would have used a blend of toxic lead white that, not long after the artist's death, we know began to change.

Year after year, dust dimmed its glow and actual light bleached the painted scene. Tiny cracks in the pigment began to spread, and eventually the piece would need to be fumigated with formaldehyde after woodworms devoured the cherry-wood frame. By the time it was determined that its transfiguring light needed to be restored to what it once had been, it was fly-specked and had been slathered in a noxious, damaging varnish that someone had mistakenly believed would let the light carry on and on.

∽

The purest white?

Forget what you think you know. There's a piece by Kate comprised of nothing but blank sheets of paper, arranged in loose folds, spiraling down from the ceiling. Or there's the white of her *Pillow Busts*, a series of halved pillowcase casts made all the more white through their arrangement on pedestals painted sky blue. Each bust, with its own unique crease and curve, lilt and sag and dimpled spot where a head once lay, seems to embody the concept of "pillow" as a Platonic ideal.

At the same time, each one begins not to seem pillow-like at all, resembling instead billowing sails, fossilized clouds, or ancient torsos sanded and smoothed until some abstract essence of body is achieved and the sculpture teems, simmers, dazzles, and brims the way Rilke described that bust of Apollo.

Perhaps that's a story you know: after watching Rodin pound and chisel marble slabs each day, Rilke vowed to stop gauzing his work with abstract emotions and instead to tether his poems to

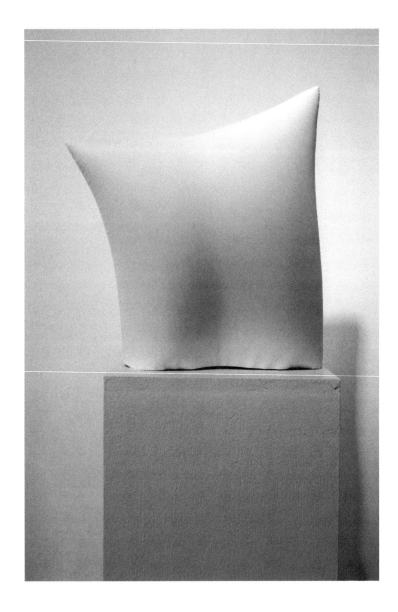

things. After first tackling a panther striding behind bars at the Paris zoo, he turned to that statue at the Louvre where the torso "is still suffused with brilliance from the inside, / like a lamp, in which his gaze, now turned to low, / gleams in all its power." Or, Rilke writes, also allowing his similes to accrue, it glistens like a wild beast's fur, like a burst star's fires. If the comparisons don't quite mesh, it matters little in the end; instead, it's the sheer act of looking that fuels the statue's imagined voice in those fierce last words: "You must change your life."

Whenever I look at Kate's work, I feel some paraphrase of that blindsiding command, not because her art seeks the kind of thunderous oracular voice that Rilke's gazed-upon statue employs, but because her distillation of process, her seriousness of intent, her tenacious acts of looking, put my own flailing attempts at making to shame. Today, enraged by the fact of her illness, I go further still: given how they never seem to sit in silence, then sit and look some more, given how, in all our tales, they transform and take, avenge and glide, choose when to heal and when to cure nothing at all, I tell you it's the gods whose lives must change.

The Latin inscription over Raphael's tomb in the Pantheon is well known: "Here lies that famous Raphael by whom Nature feared to be conquered while he lived, and when he was dying, feared herself to die." Less clear is how to respond to its lies.

Where to begin? With investing Nature with human pettiness and mortal fears? With that implied privileging of one life above all others?

Or perhaps with the inscription's mischaracterization of Raphael's work as just a mirroring of the natural world. Believe me: this is no art-speak quibble. If some of his paintings give back sun-teeming branches or a wind-pummeled cloud, there is of course more to tell.

After the discovery of Nero's palace—an unexcavated ruin that had remained essentially intact—artists would pilgrimage to a hole in the earth and descend by rope into long-buried rooms in order to view wall paintings the ancients had left behind. Raphael, too, was lowered in several times, and made use of many of those shape-shifting forms for his painting of the Vatican's arches, ceilings, and walls. In that decorative work—"grotesques," we call them—red vines loop into angels that curlicue into taffy-like griffins with donkey-eared heads that sprout into fountains or perhaps feathery lozenges knotted to garlands laced around a bridge composed of bone-shaped bricks.

Thus yet more poorly lit, inscrutable beauty, yet more lawless whim.

⤳

During a window of time in which Kate felt well enough to see friends, we drove by her house again, delivering a loaf of bread, a spinach quiche, half a dozen yellow tulips. She greeted us at the door wearing a self-knitted yarn cap snug on her now-bald head, and seemed frail but also luminous in a way I wouldn't have imagined. For the first time since her diagnosis, her doctor was pleased with the latest rounds of tests. In that moment, she seemed chatty, wanting to gossip, catch up, ask about our newly adopted coonhound. And she wanted to describe her chemotherapy sessions, how they were using platinum to attack the cancerous cells. Whenever she felt well enough, she said, she'd take short walks, thinking about what it means to have that kind of radiance coursing through her blood.

⤳

I should confess that I have little love for *The Transfiguration*. At the same time, I haven't been able to relinquish it either.

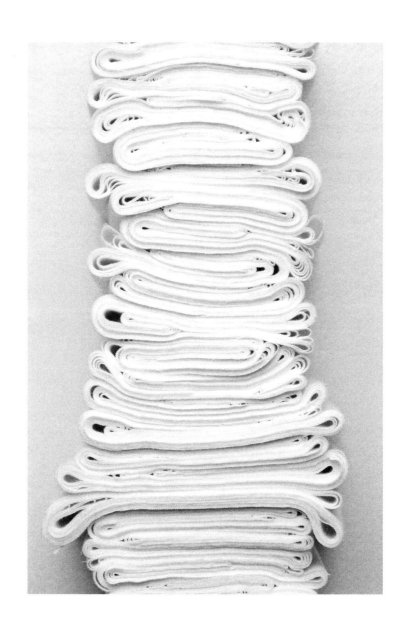

For a while, because the painting remained incomplete at the time of Raphael's death at the age of thirty-seven, I was drawn simply to the idea of the artist's last testimony as well as those tales of all of Rome bereft, grieving for the young artist's passing. The city's streets were filled with long lines of mourners, I'd read, processing to his tomb at the Pantheon where that last work had been positioned above his head. I imagined how *The Transfiguration*'s light would have been twinned by the light beaming down from the Pantheon's oculus, and how, in both the building and the painting, there would have been an illuminated mortal crowd.

For a while, this forged a correspondence that I couldn't resist. That is, until coincidence and trope did nothing to console or change the news about Kate, and the conceit came to mean nothing at all, and all that was left was the thought of flesh that needed to be cured as light spilled in relentless luster.

᠅

"I want my process to reveal the material," Kate writes, "rather than transform it."

Which is exactly what she's done with a new piece that's an untitled stack of white fabric she's mounted on a gallery wall. It's a slender column of uneven lengths of cloth that fold back on themselves. Some strips are layered in loose, untidy loops, some are tucked in tight.

Muslin Coil promises nothing more than the shape and color and texture that it is—line and curve, pattern and lapse, two meandering edges that begin a few feet up from the floor and, hard-earned, rise up a few feet more.

Kate, I'm thinking, is right yet again: the piece, it would seem, changes nothing at all. But here at last is cloth revealed as cloth, here is white as white. Here are things blazing with the way things are.

Toward Some Blossoms More or Less

⟿

"For the enjoyment of the cherry blossoms," I'm told Bashō wrote, "you must approach them with a vacant mind, free from business worries or other domestic cares." And yet, confronted by that sky-swarming, branch-sagging abundance, how might emptiness be maintained? Or, to ask it another way, when does the hard-earned depleted mind inevitably begin to fill?

"More than ever I want to see / in these blossoms at dawn / the god's face," Bashō declares in one fervent haiku. In this version of meditative gazing, the viewer's own desires teem as much as any shaggy cluster of blooms, and any potential return to a blank slate is anticipated by a fired-up, ongoing surge of grappling after the divine.

⟿

After Eliza Scidmore—world traveler, Oberlin graduate, self-designated ambassador of all that's beautiful in the East—nagged and prodded for twenty-two years; after First Lady Helen Taft, even while recovering from a stroke, plunged in and spurred things on ("I do not like this thing of being silent," she wrote to her husband about her aphasia, "but I do not know what to do about it"); after the Tidal Basin's existing oaks and elms were axed, steam-shoveled, and hauled off; after the Department of Agriculture revealed the first shipment of trees were infested with insects, fungi, and tumor-like growths; after a presidential order that all the gifted trees be burned; after a brisk flurry of editorials condemning Taft's botched diplomacy following his confession that the gifted trees were destroyed ("Occasions do arise when Truth is willing to endure a twinge or two rather than make herself disagreeable," wrote the *New York Times*); after two more years of arbitration and, quite frankly, greasing the right wheels; after tree upon tree was pulled from plots of rarefied Tokyo soil and bound on a Pacific steamship; after they clattered, knotted in place, across the United States in temperature-controlled boxcars; and after a few men heaved the swaddled root ball into a pre-dug hole and the First Lady scooped up and scattered some dirt, the first of three thousand Japanese cherry trees was planted in Washington, D.C.

That day in Potomac Park, only four dignitaries were present to watch Helen Taft tamp down the earth with the back of her shovel, then present a bouquet of American Beauty roses to the Japanese ambassador's wife. The ceremony, inspiring haiku-like compression, barely received sixty words of notice in the *Washington Post* and was summarized by the rather unassuming headline "Mrs. Taft Plants a Tree." "The idea," the article concluded, "is to have a grove on the speedway."

But the idea was so much more. Mrs. Taft, in seizing the blossom mantle, wanted the trees to "form masses, or continuous lines of bright color." She wanted cloudy tufts of pink to pack the Tidal Basin, creating a place that was "a sort of fairyland of music, gayety, and athletics." Many hoped the blooming cherries would utterly transform a rather desolate urban park. "Bring on the Cherry Trees," one editorial urged, and all their "umbrageous beauty."

⌐

Bashō wrote his dawn-blossom haiku at Mount Kazuraki during a seven-month journey west of Edo and included it in his *Knapsack Notebook*, a travelogue that interweaves prose and poetry. Although there's certainly a way in which the poem can be understood in English, the more I read about its context, insular references, and the vicissitudes of translation, the more I feel there's not much hope of approaching at least the blossoms of that haiku with the counseled vacant mind.

Some scholars suggest the poem references Hitokotonushi, a mythical Japanese god who had a shrine on Mount Kazuraki, and who was known to be mercilessly ugly; because Bashō here seeks the grotesque amid the ravishing, it may suggest the need for beauty to be coupled with whatever is unbearable to witness. Others have insisted the poem is more erudite still, referencing the specific attributes of

Hitokotonushi, whose name means "the god of one word." There is disagreement, however, as to whether the deity would only hear prayers condensed to a single utterance, or if the god himself would proclaim oracles of good or evil distilled to one word.

⌒

In Japan, I'm told, blossoms are never merely blossoms but rather an embodiment of all that's fleeting. The Japanese word *sakura* means "cherry blossom" but also means "evanescence," and its connotations are forever stitched to the principle of *mono no aware*, which, I'm told, requires a lifetime to learn but means, most literally, "a sensitivity to things." Or it may mean the very "Ah-ness" of things, which suggests an epiphany about the essence of being or, more specifically, about the loss inherent in all things. The Latin phrase *Lacrimae rerum*, which may be the closest Western equivalent to *mono no aware*, means "the tears of things" but has also been translated from *The Aeneid* as "tears haunt the world" and "they weep . . . for how the world goes."

⌒

In a photograph taken during their trans-Pacific travels accompanying the trees, both Sutemi Chinda, wearing a dapper bowler, and Iwa Chinda, towering above her husband, hands disappearing in a muff, look stricken, as if recoiling from something the viewer can't see. It's impossible to know what that first still-to-bloom tree afforded the Japanese ambassador and his wife, if only because, four years earlier, one of their sons had died, along with two hundred other soldiers, in an explosion aboard the battleship *Matsushima* while anchored in the harbor of Makang.

⌒

Matsushima ah!
Ah, Matsushima, ah!
Matsushima, ah!

In a form that often hinges on reticence, this is perhaps the most reticent of all haikus. Yet it's also a poem of exuberance that, circumventing the need for translation, enacts a Zen epiphany. (For many years, the lines were erroneously attributed to Bashō.) Confronted by the world's resplendent beauty, it seems to suggest, what more could possibly be said?

Yet now that I've read about the Chindas' son killed aboard a ship that happened to share a name with those pine-crowded islands— Matsushima—I can't help but load this haiku with an entirely different context, transforming each scored "ah" from a gasp of ineffable grace to grief that transcends words.

↬

Sunt lacrimae rerum, Aeneas says to Achates, his journeying companion, as they stand before a set of stumbled-upon pictures that depict the war in Troy. Shipwrecked on the Libyan coast, robes stiff with salt, Aeneas steadies himself in an unfinished temple to Juno, gazing upon images of the same battles and slaughter he has newly escaped. He sees tents wet with blood, bodies dragged through dirt, a woman weeping at the sky.

"What spot on earth," Aeneas asks, overwhelmed, "is not full of the story of our sorrow?"

↬

Instead of using a single word—"body"—at the opening of *Knapsack Notebook*, Bashō signifies the human form through a phrase both more literal and circuitous. "Among these hundred bones and nine orifices, there is something," Bashō's essay begins. The phrase is borrowed from the *Zhuangzi*, a cornerstone Taoist text that I cannot claim to have understood. And yet, perhaps I can still grasp Bashō's opening gesture: the body is distilled to its barest essence—bones, orifices—before the speaker trails off, uncertain what exactly to claim. And then, taking a cue from the delicate banana leaf (what his chosen name of Bashō means), he seizes upon one thing about the human form that seems beyond question: "Surely we can say it's thin, torn easily by a breeze."

↬

In March 1912, just a few days before watching Helen Taft lift her skirt's hem, grip a shovel, and plant a tree, Viscount Sutemi Chinda, Japanese ambassador to the United States, gave a speech at New York's Hotel Astor in which he declared that it was "impossible to conceive" any conflict could arise between America and Japan that couldn't be settled amicably. Latching onto a metaphor to illustrate his point, Ambassador Chinda declared that the relationship between the two countries was "not like a hothouse plant that has to be forced into flowering artificially." This particular blooming, it seems, was entirely natural.

Accompanying the cherry trees on their long journey from Japan to Washington, Chinda's optimism had been even more ebullient. Somewhere in Chicago, standing close to freight cars filled with branches yet to blossom, he spoke to the press with authority. "War has had its day," he declared.

↬

Were some god, in 1912, to whisper in the ambassador's ear but a single utterance of evil still to come in the world, what one word would you guess it might choose? There is, after all, nearly the entire twentieth century to consider, parse, weigh.

↬

Just after a haiku about fleeting dreams and octopus traps beneath the summer moon, Bashō, at the conclusion of *Knapsack Journal*, writes about the grief he hears in the sound of ocean waves. The poet is overlooking a bay where, hundreds of years before, one clan slaughtered another. This shore, he writes, is no mere shore; rather, the sorrow of a thousand years lingers on that beach. And according to legend that persists today, all the scuttling crabs are no mere crabs but resurrected spirits of the dead.

April 1185. Smoke rises from the village of Ichinotani and homes topple into cinders. The surf is crimson and jostles with cushions, samurai banners, robes flung from the imperial barge. And, according to *The Tale of the Heike* (which goes on to compare this particular death to autumn blossoms flung from branches), the eight-year-old emperor lies somewhere in the sea's depths after he was seized and drowned by his own grandmother in order to avoid capture.

⤳

A handful of days after Helen Taft plants a tree, there is little talk of cherry blossoms. The R.M.S. *Titanic*, unsinkable with its watertight hull, has sunk deep into the North Atlantic.

And yet, guided by Bashō, or rather the way we seem to grieve, I wonder when the talk turned back to blossoms. When were the dead—let's be honest—forgotten, and that sea of blooming approached with a vacant mind once more?

⤳

Bashō, it turns out, may never have said those words about blossoms and a scrubbed-free mind. Despite having encountered the line as a direct quotation by the poet, I can't locate the original source. Although it may be buried deep within other writings (I don't read Japanese), several Bashō scholars told me that they've never encountered it. More to the point, it was explained, emphatically, that the phrase "business worries" just didn't sound like the poet, and that the sentiment reeked of generic Zen advice. Apparently there's a long history of scribes and disciples either mistakenly attributing quotations to Bashō or, as a deliberate means of promoting their own ideas, publishing their own work under the master's name. In effect, Bashō

could be treated as a blank slate upon which many things might be inscribed.

⤳

Many of the Japanese names of cherry trees are difficult to translate, but most are meant to somehow describe the color or effect of each particular bloom, for which, it seems, no single word is adequate. *Imperial Yellow Costume. Tiger's Tail. The Milky Way. The River of Heaven.* The name of one tree translates to *Silence*, or *Postscript*, or perhaps even *Slander.* One means *The Royal Carriage Turns Again to Look and See.*

As Bashō exclaims in one haiku that we know with certainty he wrote, "How many, many things / they bring to mind— / cherry blossoms!"

⤳

A plaque bolted to a nondescript stone sits equidistant from the western edge of Kutz Bridge and, at least on the thawing February day I

visited the site, a homeless man's pitched tent and tarp-covered heap of belongings back within a cluster of shrubs.

A patch of mud extends from the stone's base like a late-morning shadow, and the four corner screws holding the plaque in place are designed to resemble budding flowers. There are no words describing Eliza Scidmore's first blissed-out postcard sent from Japan, or smoldering pyres of hacked-up branches, or—what did I expect?—what happened to the first tree planted by Helen Taft that it seems was lost long ago.

⌇

Say the word "tree," and what do you picture?

Cottonwood inscribed with "Skank loves Ditty," a child's bottle-green drawing of a curlicue cloud-shape perched on a slender stem? A yellowing, moth-tattered buckeye passed on a daily commute, a whole hillside of skeletal pines?

And what about Eden's forbidden branches? As a child in Sunday school, I used to try to imagine what that post-pluck moment was like for Adam and Eve. When exactly did the sweet taste of pulp give way to knowing what human hands might do? What was it like to stand in the shade of Paradise, instantly wielding new verbs?

Men planted cherry trees along the Potomac and Tidal Basin for seven years, a fact that sounds like the stuff of biblical legend. Soon after, painters, photographers, and tourists arrived in droves each spring to stand beneath the blossoms. And after the last of the three thousand were packed into earth, a small group of schoolchildren reenacted Helen Taft's planting of the first tree, which led to commissions, committees, protective laws, and the annual three-day National Cherry Blossom Festival. Which led to Miss Rose Colliflower, accompanied by red-glowing flares and sixteen canoes, being paddled in a swan boat across the near-frozen basin and crowned as the first festival queen. ("My loyal subjects," she declared in a short speech to the crowd, "We extend to Washington and her visitors the hospitality of our land of cherry blossoms and command you to admire them and enjoy them until the last petal has fluttered to the earth.") In 1941 the festival's chosen theme was defense and national preparedness, and that year, a few days after the bombing of Pearl Harbor, someone hacked down several of the largest trees, carving "To Hell with the Japanese" on one severed trunk. The next spring, due to the war between the United States and Japan, the festival was canceled by a committee's unanimous recommendation. Although in the end commissioners weren't able to garner enough votes to change the name of the annual celebration to "The George Washington Cherry Blossom Festival," the council did assert that the "Japanese" designation of those cherry trees was nothing more than a forty-year

misnomer. They were actually from Korea's Yang Ju valley, it was decreed, and mournful symbols of aggression; they should be called, more accurately, "Oriental Flowering Cherries," and the committee officially declared that each tree was United Nations "from root to twig top."

⌒

Suspended by steel cables from a museum's ceiling, a plane is angled into a dive bomb. Next to the stenciled number fifty-nine and Japanese characters I can't read, a blocky five-point blossom is painted onto the plane's metal. In this form—the pink of its petals cribbed in by a darker, jagged border; its center composed of thinning sun-yellow arms—it resembles less a single cherry bloom than a posted warning for radiation.

The English translation of *kamikaze* is "divine wind," and the death-mission planes were called *Ohkas*, which means "cherry blossom," too. With that insignia bright on the side of those piloted missiles, the planes literally enacted the intended metaphor: *sakura*, the ephemeral, blossoms falling in wind.

⏤

In a photo, young girls hold cherry branches aloft as a kamikaze pilot prepares to take flight. Their heads are bowed and their arms lifted high as they clutch the branches. Each child is spaced a uniform distance from the other, like trees planted along a boulevard.

In a photo, a man, still in his teens, smiles at the camera. He wears a white scarf and an aviator cap, its fuzzy earflaps askew. Snapped-off branches of cherry blossoms are knotted to the front of his uniform; even more jut from his helmet, shoulders, and back. He looks, for all the world, not like a man about to fly a plane to his death but a boy who has just stumbled from the underbrush, scuffed with forest debris.

⏤

The first time I heard about the bombing of Hiroshima, I was barely listening. Our teacher read some statistics, showed us photographs of the city's flattened remains, and spoke about the necessity of ending the war. The only thing I remember actually hauling home that day was a single passing detail: at the moment of the bomb's impact, the heat was so intense that fields of sweet potatoes, still growing beneath the earth, were roasted whole. Of all the things I might have latched onto, news of the plant world was somehow manageable.

⏤

Just before Aeneas proclaims about the tears of things, he strolls through the new riches of Carthage. He gapes at the piers, pillars, cobblestone streets, dredged harbors, and a new temple begun on the precise spot where someone found the sculpted head of a warhorse,

which could only be a sign, the Carthaginians believed, of an easy, plentiful life. The city so teems, Virgil tells us, it was like watching the workings of a hive—thyme-scented air alive with movement, flurries of pollen-heavy bodies, fresh honey oozing from the home.

~

Fly to Washington, D.C., during the National Cherry Blossom Festival, and it might help to call 1-800-44BLOOM in order to find accommodation. Find yourself with a few hundred bucks to burn, and you can choose between blossom lapel pins, key chains, magnets, mugs, brooches, twenty-four-ounce aluminum water bottles, tote bags, a pink-hued NCBF pen, or a tie decorated with what resembles less budding petals than a school of garish jellyfish pumping their bodies east.

During the blossom festival, forget evanescence: "More is more" is the operative spirit of those three days. Watch the one-mile parade weaving down Constitution Avenue, and you'll see waxed hot rods,

Minnie Mouse in a kimono, sumo wrestlers, the Blossom Queen cruising in a float with her fourteen-karat crown embedded with fifteen hundred pearls, an enormous cross-legged, helium-leaking Kermit hovering above the Supreme Court, and gaggles of beaming Washington Wizard cheerleaders leg-thrusting in sync. And in addition to the thick blossoms billowing the trees, you'll see blossoms that have become colossal salmon-colored balloons, each requiring a half-dozen grinning parade volunteers to keep them from tumbling off into the sky, each in the shape of something blossom-like but also resembling a garden spigot knob, or a puffy wad of candy, or some ambiguous internal organ.

↝

Bashō, upon viewing the cherry blossoms of Mount Yoshino, decided not to write a haiku after all, despite having traveled for two years in order to see them. "Words would not come," he wrote, "and I could only close my mouth."

One kamikaze pilot, airborne and soaring toward his target, just before being summoned back to base due to a brewing storm, described "a strange sense of freedom from all thoughts and ideas."

↝

Twenty months after atomic bombs fell on Hiroshima and Nagasaki, D.C.'s blossom festival began once again, a fact that few at the time seem to have thought worth inscribing with much meaning. That same year, two weeks away from "blossom-time," officials remained concerned about freezing temperatures and belated snows and the risk of sold-out hotels. "Life," one headline read, "Is No Bowl of Cherries for Blossom Festival Heads."

↝

In 1947 the festival's first postwar theme is World Peace. As part of the celebration, planes soar in loose formation and drop cherry blossoms on the crowd.

Plummeting from the sky, the blossoms fall onto grass and the road's cool stones and drift in wet clumps in the Potomac. Some rain down onto the clothes and hair of those milling below, and some snag in the flower-heavy branches of the trees, blanketing blossoms with even more blossoms still. There is no one word to describe it—they fall like some impossible, scuttling rain, in long veils or fluttering sheets or waves of something unnamable that seems to go on and on.

Almost a Full Year of Stone, Light, and Sky

⤳

He could see the white-washed rocks; the tower, stark and straight; he could see that it was barred with black and white; he could see windows in it; he could even see washing spread on the rocks to dry. So that was the Lighthouse, was it?

No, the other was also the Lighthouse. For nothing was simply one thing. The other Lighthouse was true too. It was sometimes hardly to be seen across the bay. In the evening one looked up and saw the eye opening and shutting and the light seemed to reach them in that airy sunny garden where they sat.

—VIRGINIA WOOLF, *To the Lighthouse*

If you're gazing out over the Rome skyline on the Gianicolo hill, sipping a kiosk's lukewarm six-euro beer, you'll see it, there among the brick buildings and sky-jabbing cupolas and the city's infinite shades of Tang, hunkered down with all the grace of an up-turned cereal bowl.

Down the hill, there are two means of approaching it. You could weave in from one of the side streets to the north until you round some darkened bend and there it is, smack-dab across the Piazza della Rotunda in a *ta-da* all-at-once splendor. Far better, though, is the slow-reveal afforded by strolling in from the south. Step from

the number eight tram and meander through nameless side streets chockablock with scooters, tour groups, double-parked trucks, pallet stacks, purse shops, and prix fixe restaurants. Take your time. What you'll see is only a beginning, a partial glimpse, a long curve slowly taking shape like an oversized misplaced brick silo. Its familiar pillars and dome will be nowhere in sight. For as long as possible, allow what you know you know to be held at a distance even as it's within reach.

↶

Pantheon, we say, hauled in from the Greek: *pan*, meaning "all," and *theon*, meaning "of the gods." More than anything else, this etymology is how we've come to agree—or wrongly guess—that this building was a place to worship all Roman gods during ancient times. Yet, like everything else we inhabit or inherit, neither its name nor its function is that simple.

After its conversion to a Christian church in the seventh century, the building became officially known as Santa Maria ad Martyres. More informally, it's called Santa Maria della Rotonda, whereas all of Rome's brown historic-site signs direct visitors to "Il Pantheon." Yet that name, even in ancient times, seems to have been more of an agreed-upon nickname. Dio Cassius, although he was writing not long after the building was constructed, finds himself scrambling to account for why it was known as the Pantheon. Perhaps it has to do with all the statues of the gods the building once housed, he writes, but ventures his own opinion too: perhaps it has to do with the fact that its vaulted roof resembles the heavens in which all of the gods reside.

In the end, no one knows its original name, or how it might have been possible to worship all our myriad gods within one building, or if the building was ever in fact holy at all.

〜

While its interior is composed of seemingly endless architectural details to explore—trompe l'oeil niches, contrapuntal marble, the dome's concrete coffers high above—some have argued that its basic exterior structure is like that of a prototypical house. At one point, I remember looking at it from across the piazza dead-on and seeing at long last what they meant: ignore the pillars and the dome's visible sliver, and you have a square with a triangle on top.

This is how my son Cyrus drew his first home not long after learning to clutch a pencil, and, years later, this is more or less how he carved a house-like shape into his Etch-a-Sketch's dark sand by rotating those little white knobs. But no matter if he's using a periwinkle Crayola or a nub of red chalk to inscribe his walls upon the walls of our home, his square capped with a triangle hat is mostly just a means of getting at the stories held within those shapes. He'll finish his drawing, squint at its lines as if peering inside, then improvise

tales about who lives there, who built it, what its pebble-bottom fish tanks and damp cellars are like. What he's made is just a shell, a vessel, a starting point for riffing on whatever might transpire inside.

⌒

A few years back, I received a fellowship that allowed me to spend eleven months in Rome. It was a blissful time: essentially free of commitments, I spent whole days wandering the city and writing about whatever caught my eye. There was no plan beyond hunting down some sought-after thing—a painting, a fountain, a particular trattoria's mozzarella-oozing zucchini blossoms, some wind-whipped Bernini marble furl. I could stumble across a guidebook reference to a rarely seen Last Judgment fresco, for instance, and, by midmorning the following day, spill from an elevator into a church's choir loft and find myself standing before its radiant slew of haloed apostles and angels. Back at my desk, I might jot notes about wings like fountains of flames, or perhaps instead tackle the surly mustached nun who had chaperoned my fresco pilgrimage and flicked the room's lights on and off after I'd lingered too long.

"No one suspects the days to be gods," Emerson wrote, but for the short window of that time in Rome, I had faith in little else. The city was inexhaustible, and some of those days, by god, revealed themselves to be unfathomable, awe-crammed things. No matter what I pursued, seized, flitted past, devoured, or stood stupefied before, there was always a wonder-packed still-more to pounce upon the next day.

Gradually, though, the Pantheon became an exception to all this wafting. I began to reroute my roaming so that, no matter my far-flung agenda, I'd be able to walk once more beneath its dome. As my time in the city neared its end, I found myself forgoing the chance to visit another work of art or new-to-me ruin so that I'd be able to carve out whole afternoons—or even five minutes—to sit in that building's bustling cool, to glimpse where its light happened to fall, to check if its revealed patch of sky happened to be cloud-pocked or spotless blue.

"What is this quest all about?" a friend finally asked me, yet in all of my repeat visits to the building, I never had much of a defined pursuit. For better or worse, my compulsive returns were something akin to Philip Larkin's "Church Going," in which the narrator stops by churches just to poke around, never quite sure what he's seeking. It's a dabbling fueled by a loss of faith, although he never locates an alternative to belief. Instead of doctrine, there's the hum of desire and an ill-defined tethering. There's the lure itself and the way "someone will forever be surprising / A hunger in himself to be more serious, / And gravitating with it to this ground."

I must admit that I was surprised by my accruing hunger for the Pantheon and how my own lurching compass settled there. After months of searching out churches in Rome—the city boasts over nine hundred—why did this one structure trump all others? After visiting ruin upon ruin, what did this one ancient place—not a ruin, against all odds—offer, suggest, redeem?

↫

"I found another spear!" Oliver shrieks, deeply pleased that along our afternoon walk he's discovered yet another stainless-steel pole jutting up from New Mexico dirt.

Given that there are 400 such poles, each spaced precisely 220 feet apart and arranged in meticulous rows within a mile-wide rectangular grid, and given that we'd been clumping through Walter De Maria's *Lightning Field* installation for more than an hour already, the presence of these "spears" shouldn't have come as a surprise to my three-year-old. And yet there was something infectious about his pride and delight, as if perpetual astonishment was the only suitable response to all that slender and unlikely sheen. As if the last thing on the mind of someone wandering that space should be any of the back-story facts crammed onto the laminated pages available in the cabin at the site: engineering surveys, photogrammetric work, laser scans, and a list of the thirty-two companies (ranging from Acme Tube to Yellow Bird Inc.'s helicopter services) that had been contracted to help with the business of cutting, welding, grinding, lathing, polishing, and positioning 8,651 feet of 2-inch type 304 stainless-steel tubing into that barren sprawl.

If you've ever visited; if you've reserved your twenty-four-hour slot in order to be one of six people allowed to stand in that place and witness the way those poles seem both entirely estranged and wholly inseparable from the landscape they inscribe; if you've swayed beneath that light, staring across to the Sawtooth Mountains, wondering how each of those rods can seem urgent even as the horizon is packed with what look like meager brushstrokes guiding the eye toward nothing but clouds wafting sky; if you've ever wandered with a bellyful of Cracked Earth aka Chocolate Chess Red Chile Pie after an earlier pit stop at the nearby Pie-O-Neer and felt your worldly desires pruned to a thirst for lightning to descend; if you've peered from the site's cabin window, saddled with supervising the now pole-weary kids, relegated to that tantalizing threshold, gazing across to the work and desperate to be back within it, then you can bung the binder filled with decimals and measurements and all that how-it-was-done debris and instead plunge straight into De Maria's rare plainspoken claim a few pages in: "The sum of the facts does not constitute the word or determine its esthetics." Or, as he declares a few lines down, "The invisible is real," a "huh?"-worthy phrase if ever there was one, except that ever since you tramped across that field, you must admit that you know what he means.

↬

And what facts do we need, how far back must we go, to comprehend the Pantheon's particular light? Even if mostly I'm content to simply experience the span of its dome and the sun's flare on its stone, it's still worth remembering why the building sits on that particular *there*.

Some say you need to cast a gaze all the way back to Romulus, the fratricidal co-founder of Rome. The Pantheon stands, it's believed, on the exact spot where he either ascended into heaven on a golden chariot like a slingshot-fired jewel or he was ambushed along the marsh's edges by a gang of knife-wielding senators who hacked his body to pieces, then scattered them in the lake.

And some say you need to know how Julius Caesar wanted to give thanks to Mars after winning four wars, which really meant needing to appease his soldiers with extravagant parades as well as distract the public from all those years he sucked the coffers dry. Thus elephants, chariots, prisoners of war, drunk officers bellowing victory songs, and war booty lugged past cheering crowds that held aloft drawings of Cato tearing at his own wound. Thus *Veni, vidi, vici* and five days of beast fights and the first-ever staged hunts for giraffe. Thus gladiatorial battles with tridents, wooden shields, axes and nets, followed by armies of hundreds of men spearing and slashing, because this is what the crowd wanted to see. Or so they thought, until the spectacle was upped a notch with naval battles in a basin built near one of the Tiber's bends where ships carrying thousands of men—some serving as proxy gallant Romans, some relegated to Tyrian scum—rammed and stormed and bludgeoned each other with oars.

Years after slaves filled in the basin where those mock battleships had sailed, Marcus Agrippa, in a bold claim about legacy and honor, choose this exact location to build a temple to the God of War. That temple burned down—we know little else about it—and later was constructed again before burning down once more before Hadrian, in turn, chose that same spot for his dome to end all domes.

Thus the light we gather to see.

↬

Just as dawn began, I happened to wake in the cabin at *The Lightning Field*. I listened to make sure that my kids were still asleep, then slipped on my boots and crept out the door without bothering to wake my wife. Selfishly, this is what I hoped for: given that we were going to experience merely a single morning at the site, I wanted that light for myself.

I quickened my steps across the desert scrub, hoping to make enough distance between myself and the cabin before someone could

holler me back to morning routines, hoping that I'd be far enough into the field to have earned a claim on that space, those poles, whatever light might come. Four rows deep, I stopped, turned to the east, and stood as still as I could.

The moment was exactly what I'd wanted, not just because it was one of those pulse-throttling mountain dawns—light pouring down through gilded clouds, the widening sky seared reddish gold—but because it belonged only to me. For as long as my friends and family slept, I was the only one seeing it through the lens of De Maria's work, which made it seem like something I possessed.

I watched the poles begin to glow, giving back the light that now was rising, some of them returning not only the sun's flare but also a deepening, improbable blue. A bird I couldn't name hovered and perched, hovered and perched, flitting from pole to pole, some of which began to glow at their tips before one of them—in a trick of the light I can't explain—seemed to lose its lower half while its top wavered and twitched like a single human hair. Coyotes screeched and yapped from behind two sets of hills, and the poles bloomed with a watery pink and a blue that darkened even more as I approached until I realized that what was reflected in the metal's gleam wasn't the sky at all but rather a smudgy, denim-dark, spear-shaped me.

Which eventually makes me think of a sky that no one claimed to own.

"Out of the clear blue," we say, meaning, of course, a blindsiding, but also meaning, given the sheer fact of this cliché, that we understand the pristine can be violated at any time.

For a long time after September 11, the attacks were rarely described without some reference to the sky's blue.

> "It was not just blue, it was a light, crystalline blue, cheerful and invigorating."

> "A late-summer sky so astoundingly blue it made the whole Northeast sparkle."

But our inability to relinquish the color of the New York sky on that September day isn't merely about our shock that an act of horror could be played out against a backdrop of sun-splayed sky. No one, of course, was claiming the day would have been any different had there been a socked-in downpour or even a few clouds lurking above the Hudson.

Then what was it?

Perhaps it has something to do with the collision between the horrific and the immaculate, how neither seemed as if it could be contained. Remember? The towers burned, and then collapsed, and smoke poured into that boundless sky—there was nothing to contain it—and both the ruin and that blue seemed unending.

❦

When the building's dome was first constructed, its interior was painted azure, and each ribbed coffer had anchored in its center an enormous bronze rosette. Perhaps this is what Shelley was referencing when, in one of his many letters sent from Rome, he described the Pantheon as "the visible image of our universe."

Many believe the dome was intended to represent the heavens, with those rows of twenty-eight recessing trapezoidal coffers signifying the Romans' twenty-eight-day lunar cycle, the painted blue representing the sky, and the rosettes serving as the gleaming pinpricks of scattershot stars. Many, too, have noted the importance of the number sixteen within the building (sixteen granite pillars support the portico, while eight apses combined with eight exedras encircle the building's interior), inviting speculation that the building references Etruscan cosmology, in which the heavens are separated into sixteen different dwelling spaces for the gods.

When I first heard about this ancient division of the skies, I imagined each god hunkered down and unable to leave their prescribed

territory, abiding by rules not that dissimilar from my hometown's Peewee Soccer games, when we were forced to stay put in our assigned painted grid on the field, waiting for the ball to roll past by chance or else face the shrill-whistle wrath of a hypervigilant dad referee. But despite the pretense of those designated spaces, the Etruscans knew both their gods and our world too well to claim that any one portion of the sky could house a single deity. Forget row after row of suburban cul-de-sac cookie-cutter homes; forget any straightedged tic-tac-toe-like grid segregating X's from O's. In their theory of the heavens, Jupiter shares a plot of sky with both Good Health and Nocturnus, the God of Night. The God of War rooms with the God of Freshwater, and Wisdom resides with Discord. Fortune bunks with a wide range of nameless crammed-in Shades, and, out in the cosmos further still, rogue deities called the Zoneless dwell, bound by nothing at all.

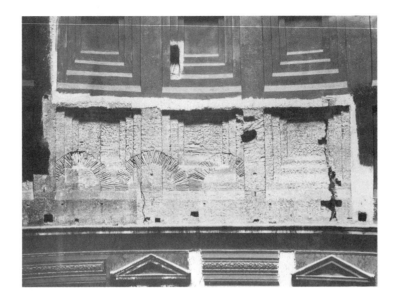

Even if Shelley knew nothing of the Etruscans' scrambled-up world of the divine, by the time he strolled through the Pantheon's doors, the dome's blue paint had long since crumbled away, and each of those rosettes' star-blaze stands-ins had been hacked off and filched many Rome-raids back, leaving those stair-step coffers to serve as frames for merely more cracked cement. *The visible image of our universe?* Shelley's description might have been intended as shorthand for limitless skylark-esque soaring, but the proxy cosmos he actually saw would have been age-pocked and scabbed with decay and long since hacked for its metal.

∽

Last night, a dream: somewhere on the snow-covered streets of Boston, I had misplaced my son. One moment, he held my hand, and the next, his palm had slipped my grip and my whole body was honed to howling his name into a January wind that whipped the drifts higher still.

I woke, sweaty and rattled, but as the day inched forward, I found myself thinking about what an anomaly the dream had seemed. In my own day-to-day life—from the classes I teach, to the night skies I scan—I rarely know what I'm looking for. I wondered, How much do I want certainty in what I seek? Do I crave more answers, facts, and faith, or, alternatively, how much of my own meandering, leapfrogging, scuttling from *and* to *if*, gives me exactly what I need?

Despite the fact that the Pantheon was converted to a Christian space long ago (and despite the crosses you'll find there), the building, I've come to believe, doesn't abide by any one creed. Unlike, say, the way a gothic spire connotes finger-pointing toward a god residing above as sure as stone, the Pantheon doesn't insist but rather reveals. Especially since we've been relegated to guesswork regarding the building's original purpose, it has become, by beautiful default, a kind of temple to speculation and wonder and thus not-knowing now and forevermore.

Here's an empty niche, a bit of light, some sky. What does it mean, what will you do with it, how will you respond?

⌒

Stendhal, apparently, viewed the Pantheon as a kind of aesthetic litmus test, judging its visitors based on their level of ravishment when exposed to its light and scale. I think I understand.

There are days when that building seems as unlikely and fantastical as anything plucked from the stuff of legend: to enter its space and not go slack-jawed would be as if you had stepped over the threshold of the Tower of Babel and responded with a shrug. Some days, yes, upon entering the Pantheon, the world narrowed to that single spot, and I felt as if I were seeing light and sky for the first time. I would be gobsmacked by that impossible dome, or merely at the thought of how many others, through nearly two millennia, had stood there as well, craning back their heads, feeling gobsmacked too.

But there were also times during my stay in Rome when I would find myself in the Pantheon while in the midst of running errands, on my way to catch the number forty-four bus, plastic sacks sagging with the weight of cantaloupe and coffee and cans of soup, and there, jam-packed among the tourists holding up iPads to the streaming-in light, I might feel as much rapture for that ancient space as I did for the squeak of wet sneakers across its marble floor.

Along those lines, although I will never doubt my son Cyrus's capacity for wonder, he could seem equally jazzed by the tower of whipped cream heaped upon his lemon granita as he was about watching light sear through that oculus. The first time he walked into the Pantheon, I watched him glance at the dome for a moment, then turn his attention to trying to decode the graphics on a sign that declared the building's prohibitions.

No tank tops, no food, no phones. Watch for pickpockets. No loud noises. No lying down.

‿っ

Ask Cyrus what he remembers most about the first time he visited the Pantheon, however, and dollars to donuts he won't mention either the light or that happened-upon sign. This is not because a barely moving ray of sunlight can't seize the mind of a five-year-old for more than a few split seconds (although this is twice-over true). Nor is it because, as he later confessed, the Pantheon's dome seemed to him like "a pretty high ceiling with a hole" (although apparently this was the case). Nor is it because his Monster Fighter Zombie Graveyard Lego set—featuring a glow-in-the-dark back-from-the-dead bride, a burly mallet-wielding Jack McHammer, and a deadly booby-trapped crypt—holds for him infinitely more engineering mysteries than the visible stack of antique bricks in the Pantheon's lower half (although this fact was underscored by the way he bolted from lower-level niche to niche, indifferent to, say, Raphael's crypt, but gushing giddily about the zombie groom that accompanied him throughout his rapid-fire tour). Rather, it's because he was blindsided by an enormous statue of an emaciated man, slender arms spread, wearing only a dirty cloth and a crown of thorns, nailed to two planks of wood. This was not only the first Crucifixion he had ever seen but, at the age of five, his first encounter with punished flesh.

Why was all he wanted to know, and there I stood beneath that patch of sky and stripped-bare dome, unsure what to say.

Remind me, if you can—I've lost my own argument's thread—how exactly my not-knowing is sacred, how my flailing trumps belief.

∽

Here is the way that Byron describes the building in its brief cameo within the sixteen thousand lines of his poem *Don Juan:* "Simple, erect, severe, austere, sublime."

While I suppose that all his adjectives are correct, in what way do any of those abstractions help depict the Pantheon? Anachronism aside, they just as easily could be describing the Eiffel Tower or, for that matter, one of the tarred railroad bridges straddling arroyo sand just a few miles from my home. Byron's brief descriptive litany, stripped of context (and, admittedly, also perhaps stripped of "erect"), seems closer to the voice-over from an SUV advertisement than to language intended to capture the Pantheon's multicolored, variegated Christian-inscribed-upon-pagan marble mash-up of the building's lower half.

At the same time, I understand the need to latch onto any ballpark word. I'm no more surprised that Byron took this broad-stroke route than that my son turned to decoding the building's rules. The Pantheon's enigmatic immensity, like all immensities, encourages whatever foothold might be found.

Sublime, severe.

No gum, no smoking, no dogs.

 ↜

Byron's stately procession of modifiers underscores not only the complications of trying to describe the place but, moreover, the way in which language has always seemed to be at odds with the structure. Words, it seems, not only fall short but also obfuscate our understanding.

Looking at the Pantheon from across the Piazza della Rotonda, it's hard to miss its famous inscription, engraved on the portico in large Roman type: M. AGRIPPA. L. F. COS. TERTIVM. FECIT. Despite the bold bronze lettering, the meaning is not much more than an ostentatious tag: "Marcus Agrippa, son of Lucius, made this building in his third consulate." For nearly two centuries, we had no reason to doubt the inscription's claim, and without fail the building was referred to as Agrippa's Pantheon. The words, however, are a lie.

In the mid-eighteenth century, bricks were excavated from various spots inside the building. Each one bore a brick-maker stamp that, through references to supply yards and names of specific supervisors, placed its construction between the years 118 and 126 A.D. and revealed that the Pantheon had been built by the Emperor Hadrian. Like that, a single fact that we thought we knew was swatted away.

My son chatters out a story about his drawing's invisible jet-powered camel that's out of sight in the backyard of his triangle-perched-upon-a-square house. Meanwhile, we've also slipped from the given to imaginative speculation: after centuries of studying the

Pantheon, our stories have shifted from the feat of Agrippa's free-standing dome to why Hadrian pretended the building wasn't his.

◡

So what happens when you stand inside the Pantheon?

The earth turns, which, depending on the time of day, makes the light appear to either rise or drop.

Light slowly cruises coffers, marble, and pillars, highlighting whatever falls beneath its path. Three bronze crosses, dust bunnies on a ledge, this particular scrap of ceiling, the man at the audio guide booth picking at his ear, now just the corn-yellow backdrop in the lower-left edge of that Annunciation scene—as if saying *notice this, so much depends*. As if beyond illuminating this skated-across mishmash of things, there was nothing more to say.

By midday in summer, it blazes on the floor, gliding over those patterned circles and squares. Some of us skirt its edge, as if we couldn't bear being caught in the glare. Some of us let the light hit us

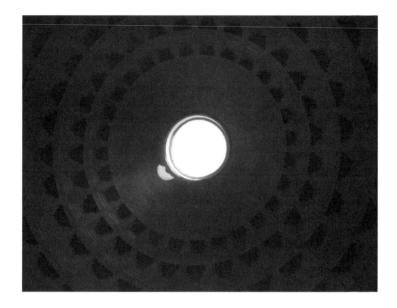

dead-on, and we stretch out our arms or strip off our socks, waggling
our toes on the sun-warmed floor, hamming it up for photos before
slipping from that blaring heat into the shadow's prescribed cool.

Come back in a few hours and the sun's beam will be rising again.
Stay long enough and—this is perhaps what we've pilgrimaged for—
the light will change as it climbs. It turns from a nearly perfect circle
shape to a crumpled disc warping across the coffers. As it lifts toward
the oculus, as each day it must, the disc becomes a cropped mountain
peak, a chewed crust of bread, a deep-hulled ship without a sail. Now
a sliver of moon, now an oblong shape inching upward for which we
have no words.

Just as the last bit of daylight hovers at the rim, giving us a glimpse
of a single cobweb strand—slung diagonal across the oculus, framed
by a backdrop disc of sky, lifting in a breeze skimming past—we're

told we must leave. A man with a lanyard looped around his neck grips the sides of the same pulpit used by the priests and solemnly intones into the microphone a sermon that goes something like this: *The building is closing. Walk toward the exit. Thank you. Please leave.*

In many languages, again and again, he tells us to go forth into the wide world. Other lanyard-bearing men and women extend their arms wide, fan out across the marble floor, and, striding toward us, make precise little flicks of the wrist, shooing us toward the exit.

In a few swift moments, the building is empty except for the guards who swing the bronze doors shut, and then we're all outside although we remain beneath the exact same light and—this is the part that's easy to forget—a wider span of the same sky. We're stepping across the piazza's bricks, past the gladiators with their plastic swords trying to shake us down for ten-euro snapshots, past the horse carriages and taxis and necking Parisians and the legless woman on a wheeled-about cart who rattles coins in her plastic cup. Past Rome tour hawkers and past two men playing a shrill Bach fugue on wineglass rims, past gangs of pigeons and gangs of guys selling splatable, water-filled pigs ("Hello. Look please! For the kids.") as our earth still turns and we seek out some just-blocks-away little hole-in-the-wall place known for its hunks of fried cod and anchovy-heaped buttered bread.

～

"Follow me," Jesus said to Matthew, and that, apparently, was that: Matthew arose and skedaddled from his old life forevermore.

But, as always for Caravaggio, this moment is less about the scripture's matter-of-fact main event—a wayward tax collector heeding a righteous call—than the light in which any heeding takes place.

In the painter's *Calling of Saint Matthew*, Jesus is there, of course, but given the way he's obscured by the shadows of the painter's trademark black, he's reduced to not much more than an extended hand, a haloed head, and, where his body should be, a few murky curves. Matthew né Levi, apostle-to-be, sits among a group of men, wearing a beret and a savage beard, responding to this hasty beckoning by cocking a finger back at himself in a stance of "Who, me?" surprise.

Or so we thought. Now that Matthew has become just another anonymous tax-greedy goon, and we've come to see that his finger doesn't gesture toward his own faux-velvet smock, but rather the even more tainted money-grubber seated at the table's end. That actual saint-to-be sits hunched over a pile of coins, not giving a gopher's fart for the light's precise burnish on the gold he clutches, nor the man who has barged in uninvited, beckoning, still standing in the doorway all these centuries later.

That painting's meticulous light is housed in the San Luigi dei Francesi Church, about four hundred feet from the Pantheon as the gray-bellied Roman crow flies. It would have been easy enough for the painter to suck up to his patrons and sentimentalize the scene with some kitschy, indisputable, God-proxy beam. As always, Caravaggio, the murderer, the brawling thug, had it right: his light, like our light, doesn't discriminate. It doesn't summon or rarify or cast apart. It floods in and slopes and spreads and tells it slant wherever it happens to fall: a splay of blank wall, the one-shutter window opening onto nothing, the tax collector's not-yet-holy left thigh, the wood of the tabletop where my namesake saint forever remains not a saint, oblivious to any finger-jabbing call.

⏤

In one of his most anthologized poems, George Herbert springboards through metaphors for prayer, flitting through half-lines that depict the act as a banquet, God's breath, reversed thunder, and the sinner's refuge before rupturing the poem's rapid-fire expansive claims—bird

of Paradise, the Milky Way, the land of spices—with two muted concluding words: prayer is, he states, "something understood," a definition I think I can grasp.

I remember sitting in the back pews of church as a kid, wondering where I should be looking. Nothing seemed to offer much. Not the wet-eyed pastor, who more than once spun a sermon that used sunscreen as a metaphor for Jesus. Not the twitching flames of the altar's candles, or the organist's bright magenta nails, or the stained shirt collar of the doughy man who always seemed to be seated in front of me. I spent many Sunday mornings mouthing hymns, futzing my way through a misremembered Lord's Prayer, standing whenever I was instructed to stand, watching field grass sway outside.

Once a year, during the celebration of Pentecost, members of the Roman fire brigade haul sacks of rose petals to the Pantheon's roof and, on cue when the mass is complete, scatter flowers through the oculus onto the tourists and congregation below. The roses are meant to be flaming tongues, or emblems of truth, or the Holy Spirit itself, none of which I can claim to understand. I only know that the firemen lounge on the Pantheon roof, smoking cigarettes and enjoying

the view until a canned recording of "Veni Creator Spiritus" blares from the speakers below and they hurl fistfuls of roses down through the ancient hole, making a crimson cascade all through the domed space from which no one in the building below turns away until all the flowers have become a brilliant blanket covering the marble floor.

Or so I'm told. I've never managed to attend the Pentecost celebration in the Pantheon, but it's no matter in the end. Even if I've never seen those once-a-year rose petals fluttering down, I've stood spellbound as rain poured through its roof, understanding, once again, nothing at all, but rather just looking at something that seemed to be wholly itself, wholly sufficient, and—surely this too is a kind of prayer—for a while not needing to guess about anything.

⌒

Nothing remained of the former structure except a porch and a marble plaque bearing his dedication to the Roman citizens; the inscription was carefully replaced, just as before, on the front of the new temple. It mattered little to me to have my name recorded on this monument, which was the product of my very thought. On the contrary, it pleased me that a text of more than a century ago should link this new edifice to the beginning of our empire, to that reign which Augustus had brought back to peaceful conclusion. Even in my innovations I liked to feel that I was, above all, a continuator.

This is how novelist Marguerite Yourcenar imagines Hadrian explaining the inscription on the Pantheon's exterior to his designated successor, Marcus Aurelius. Although there are more likely scenarios than what is conveyed here—the original dedication miraculously surviving a razing fire before being affixed to Hadrian's temple more than a century later—it's possible that Yourcenar's version of the emperor's modesty brushes shoulders with the truth. That might explain, for instance, why Hadrian dedicated numerous temples that were restored during his reign—including Neptune's basilica and the Forum—with the names of their original builders in lieu of his own.

Yet instead of stone-hard certainties, we have chiseled letters that were filled with bronze, then later hacked for the metal they contained, and, centuries later, restored with bronze yet again, remaining dubious through it all. Just below those words on the edifice, there's stone that's been carved to resemble acanthus leaves. Just above, there's a span that's blank except for pockmarks which apparently indicate the spot where a marble frieze was once clamped into place. Although to me that chisel-mark pattern looks as random as a gunfire spray, some who have studied the placement of those holes believe that the pediment was once decorated with a wing-spread eagle, framed by a large wreath and clutching in its talons a fluttering ribbon that was inscribed with nothing at all.

∽

In Brueghel's painting *The Tower of Babel*, there's an enormous rock being sculpted into a rotund, honeycombed form that seems to be beating a hasty path up through the sky. All across the tower's stone, there are pulleys, ladders, scaffolding grids, anchored ships teeming with supplies, and human-shaped specks caught midtask: they clamber and hoist, heave and scurry, point, unload and stack. Without any sign of a backhanding Yahweh to nip things in the bud—the only other thing occupying that blue is a cloud which resembles a hunchback hummingbird soaring at the painting's upper edge—the work seems as if it will go on and on.

Yet even though the painting is infinitely detailed, it explicates nothing. No matter how many times I click and zoom on zoomable versions online, squinting at reproductions of ladder rungs or pry bars

or shadows cast by the spokes of a cart's wooden wheels, I never seem to get any closer to understanding those workers' inscrutable activity. My best guess is that the job seems to involve more a process of excavation rather than brick-by-brick construction, as if, like Michelangelo's claim that each marble block has a shape waiting inside it, the earth had been cradling this mammoth heaven-scraping form all along.

I click and zoom, plunging in and in: the human-shaped specks become human-shaped smudges, the tower's rocks become nothing but feathery brushstrokes, seemingly light as air.

↬

The first time we traveled with our son from New Mexico to New York City, we stayed in a room on the hotel's twelfth floor. Each morning, he'd stand transfixed at the window, gazing down at the scuttling, miniaturized world below, squinting up at the buildings that still towered above.

"I bet if we were staying in one of those rooms up there," he announced, craning his head back, "we'd be able to lick the sky."

Perhaps something of that desire fueled the construction of our first skyscrapers: we hoped not just to leave the earth but, through inhabiting the ethereal, to literally scrape it away in the sense of the

Old Norse *scrappa*, meaning "to erase." Which is what skyscrapers do: if we can never rival the heavens, if Babel-like we will always fail to dwell beyond certain delineated heights, then we can still inscribe over the sky's expanse and thus claim it as our own.

The Pantheon, in contrast, seems to quietly propose an alternative to that kind of chutzpah-teeming upward thrust. Although admittedly most of the sky also remains concealed when one stands beneath that dome, the effect is not of having the world blotted out but, through the way in which the oculus narrows the visitor's gaze, of reminding us how little of the limitless we truly comprehend, how much of the everyday we fail to see. It's something like William Blake's "world in a grain of sand": even in that small disc of blue or cloud-packed gray, there's an elusive immensity.

A century before "skyscraper" came to denote Chicago's ten-story steel-framed Home Insurance Building in 1888, it was the name of a thoroughbred racehorse. Somewhere within those years, it meant a small sail near the top of a mast, then a thermal-winging bird, then became slang for any tall man.

⤸

Most often, whenever I have the opportunity to visit the Pantheon, I bully my way past the granite columns, past the ambling tourists bottlenecking its doors, and beeline for its interior. One brutally early morning, however, carrying a camera, a notebook, and a half-hatched plan to see what it looked like in the pre-dawn light, I deliberately visited the building when I knew that it would be closed. From the piazza's spouting sea-monster fountain, I watched the dome's arch glow as the day began. Through the crack in the building's locked doors, I could see a sliver of the roof's sliver of sky. And, perhaps by default, I lingered beneath the portico, looking at those granite columns as if for the first time.

But so what? If I traced an entire within-reach crack, or paused for a moment over a mottled blotch webbing a stone column's gray, to what end?

Each of the sixteen shafts is forty feet tall and weighs about fifty tons (roughly the same amount as an oil tanker or a newborn right whale). These columns would have been quarried at Mons Claudianus in northern Egypt, while each of the white marble footings would have come from Attica. And exactly how would all this improbable hauling take place in antiquity? No matter how many theories or descriptions I read—sledges, barges, pulleys, oxen, miles of knotted rope—I'm left mostly guessing about how these massive stones were moved from Egypt to Rome. There's also the fact that I care less about these particular facts than the sheer polysyllabic beauty of names like "Attica" and "Mons Claudianus."

All cultural treasures, Walter Benjamin wrote, owe as much to anonymous toil as the great minds in power, and all have an origin that cannot be contemplated without horror. While he's right, of course, about the relationship between authoritarian rule and so many of the beloved things of our world, I don't share his faith that all acts of pondering what we've managed to save or amass inevitably hurl us down that path.

Aren't we adept at cloistering our looking? Is it immoral to stand in horror-less awe?

As I stood beneath the portico outside the Pantheon's locked doors, I never once thought about a laborer collapsing to his knees or miles of army-scorched homes. There I was, paused, really looking, pressing a palm against one of those columns and—do you blame me?—considering not much more than the way its stone was already warm beneath that early morning sun.

◠

In 1928, after Il Duce demanded that a massive obelisk be erected in his honor, the largest marble monolith ever quarried began its 200-mile journey from the Apuan Alps to the streets of Rome. Footage on YouTube shows a casket-like box yoked to a herd of oxen, inching its way down a mountainside, creeping through village streets.

Soap-slick wooden planks had been placed along its path as a means of easing its movement. Many believe that this strategy—called the Lizzatura Method—would also have been used to transport the Pantheon's monoliths from Egypt.

Mussolini's stone weighed over 250 tons, extended more than 5 stories high, and required 8 months of heavy labor (in addition to 18,000 gallons of wood-lubricating soap) before it reached its destination. Yet despite these facts and the incredible feat of engineering its transport must have required, no one captured in the footage seems

especially troubled by the ordeal. It's as if we're watching an Italian village going about everyday tasks. The dozens of oxen don't seem to be straining at all, and many of the men carrying switches alongside the herd move with an ambling pace. As workers casually position plank after plank in front of the immense wooden crate, it slides forward with astonishing ease, making its descent seem inevitable, carefree.

There are even several shots taken after the cameraman must have climbed aboard the obelisk's box—what's the weight of one more person when you're contending with hundreds of tons?—so that we're carried along, too, airborne, gliding past homes and faces peering from windows, past the crowd that's gathered below to watch this enormous stone cruise. At one point, as the box brushes against it, a metal streetlamp bends back with the ease of someone opening a garden gate.

⌒

Noi tireremo diritto, reads the inscription in a font meant to evoke the Roman empire's world reign: "We shall go forward." Also engraved into the wall's stone beneath these boldface words is an enormous capital *M* (for Mussolini) as well as a map of Africa where some countries are claimed by conquest—Libya, Ethiopia—while much of the continent remains a wide swath of white space, blank and unnamed except for a few vein-like river squiggles.

The wall where that marble inscription can be found used to belong to a kind of fascist YMCA. Now, the space has been converted into a cinema and contemporary art space in Rome's Trastevere neighborhood, meaning that on your way to see a video of Marina Abramović slow-swaying to a tango, you'll pass below this victory map in the atrium. Rather than trying to elide the past, to change what was once etched in stone, the administrators of this art space—as a reminder? a pledge not to conceal history? as some kind of retro-chic fascist kitsch?—decided to keep it all intact.

↜

Laudate Dominum in sanctis eius read the lines from the book of Psalms that, in the eighteenth century, Pope Alexander VII had inscribed onto the lower ring of the Pantheon's so-called attic zone, just below the building's midway point. *Laus Eius in Ecclesia Sanctorum:* "Praise ye our Lord, sing his praise in the church of saints."

But these engraved words have improbably disappeared. Although the letters were chiseled in stone, they might as well have been scribbled in Tiber riverbed muck. Alexander's words didn't even last a century before they were deliberately erased during the restoration work of Paolo Posi, a semicompetent architect who was best known for his ornate festival structures that were designed to spout fireworks for a single raucous night. Those Latin words had replaced in turn a long-lost ancient Roman inscription that had also been intended to forever circumscribe the building's visitors.

Given what Alexander's quotation chose not to include from the Bible, his lines contain an elision of a different breed. Just a few verses later in the book of Psalms, talk of faith, praise, song, and joy gives way to an alternative path to glory:

> May the praise of God be in their mouths
> and a double-edged sword in their hands,
> to inflict vengeance on the nations
> and punishment on the peoples,
> to bind their kings with fetters,
> their nobles with shackles of iron,
> to carry out the sentence written against them—
> this is the glory of all his faithful people.

~

When the artist Anselm Kiefer set out to purchase the defunct, decommissioned German nuclear reactor near Koblenz, he explained his unquenchable desire in part by declaring it his personal Pantheon. "Standing in the center and looking through the hole in the middle is stunning," Kiefer claimed.

Seen in this way, anything that frames our view of the sky becomes a kind of Pantheon. A scribble of briars, a length of plastic tube, that needle eye I once held up to the cloudless blue in order to test this theory about looking.

Back in high school in Ohio, we used to play hooky at Kent State University, where we'd slow-sip bottomless mugs of coffee at Brady's Café, cough-hack our way through packs of clove cigarettes, and set up shop near the entrance doors wielding dog-eared copies of *The Fountainhead* or *The Dharma Bums* as props. If one of us hoped to wow

some fellow café rat, we'd inevitably wander over to campus to see our bullet hole.

Our bullet hole was in fact *a* bullet hole made in a metal sculpture on May 4, 1970, after National Guardsmen, armed with rifles fixed with bayonets, opened fire on students protesting the Vietnam War. Over the course of thirteen seconds on that day, sixty-seven rounds were fired, killing four students and wounding nine others. The bullets struck chests and thighs, ankles, backs, and knees. One bullet found a neck, another a mouth, and one bullet found Don Drumm's *Solar Totem #1*, a piece of public art that resembles a top-heavy house-of-cards.

In the photograph of the aftermath—so different from the gang of us, jabbing our fingers into the hole—you can see several men wearing thick-rimmed glasses, tentatively gathered around that newly made freckle of sky and light, unsure what it meant, not knowing what to do.

⮑

Throughout his reign in the mid-seventeenth century, Pope Alexander was fascinated by the Pantheon and explored numerous options for not only restoring the ancient building but also adding decorous enhancements. The Vatican archive contains sketches of a design for a new façade as well as a drawing of a fish-scale-patterned glass dome that, under the pretense of ending the rainstorms that occasionally washed out mass, would have fully sealed the building's oculus. There are proposals to embellish the coffers with bronze patterns of stars, rosettes, and oak leaves, and, in one architectural sketch, a plan to adorn the bands between them with a circumscribing rendering of the pope's own name.

We don't know exactly what became of Alexander's hopes to possess the dome by turning it into a baroque, self-aggrandizing gleam. Nor do we know what was the ultimate fate of the gadfly who set up camp under the Pantheon's portico, refusing to abide by the pope's attempt to keep the entranceway merchant-free. "For the third time," Alexander's diary records in exasperation, "let's chase that flower seller from in front of the left column."

Even if so much of the Pantheon's history has been lost, at least we've retained this one foothold into the past: that one anonymous, tenacious salesman, circling back to the portico after being threatened yet again by the pope's stick-wielding henchmen, sweat ringing the pits of his cloak, jars of yellow dwarf carnations rattling in his cart.

⮑

A friend has staged a series of performance art pieces at various locations around Rome—Ponte Sisto Bridge, Trastevere's piazza,

in front of that statue of Marcus Aurelius on a horse. In each of his videos, here, in essence, is what you see: a man wearing a blue shirt and dress pants, engaging in a series of both choreographed and improvised fidgets.

If the performances are wonderfully baffling, what's even more difficult to articulate is why his work is so moving and why his body's gestures seem to so urgently matter. In one moment, he seems to be striking a pose for a waltz, then about to backstroke through air, now steeling himself for a forward stride that never comes. His wrist pivots as if pouring a cup of tea. His body is both fluid and jerky, robotically rigid then on the verge of puddling into a heap of deboned flesh.

In the piece filmed in front of the Pantheon, he cranes his neck as if looking for something, then pauses and seems to look more still. His fingers twitch, and his arms momentarily lock into place for a tug-of-war mime that never comes. Now he's cradling empty air, then nearly remembering something before reaching for a pocket, swiveling his neck, leaning in for a doorknob that isn't there.

And still, even as I try to enact translations from body to words,

I know these literalized readings of his gestures are misguided. His motions aren't pantomimes, and to view them as such is to distort what he does, which is to enact a kind of dance that seems as emphatic as it is impregnable and forever unresolved. His performance underscores the wide gap between our individual gestures—our fevered little movements—and the monumental sublime. Although the building may be willing to harbor our desires, our erratic choreographies, it remains unaffected, indifferent to all the ways in which we're always writhing below.

⌒

Of course, there's been other light too.

Once, away from college on a summer break, sitting on the beach in San Francisco, blue-balled and sucking on the neck of a woman whom I wouldn't love for long, I caught a glimpse of the sea's horizon and—I couldn't help it—gave up the pleasures of the flesh midkiss in order to squint at the Pacific swallowing the sun, which, as if welcoming the waves' reprieve, seemed to pick up its pace and promptly disappeared with an inexplicable last-hurrah burst of green.

Once, after a wayward rufous-necked wood rail somehow missed the turn for the rank jungles of Belize and ended up in the United States for the first time, I drove to New Mexico's Bosque del Apache, hoping to see its bright-blue nape skittering through the cattails. No such luck, except for the luck that was the light falling on the hills and gangly flocks of sandhill cranes, on the bundled-up birders and the glass-like lake that trumped my need to notch the belt with a fluke glimpse of the bubblegum-pink legs of a crayfish-stalking rail.

Once, breezing past in the Met, I was seized by Edward Hopper's *Tables for Ladies*, how the light smutches and streaks that restaurant's window display. In that canvas's ripe land of plenty—so different from the stark emptiness in which most Hopperites dwell—it grazes the still-corked champagne, the fake ferns and pork chops on ice, the grapefruits lined like a bead of pearls, and the collarbone of the woman leaning in, fiddling with the fruit basket in order to ensure it catches the best light.

And once—to round out what is also a cherry-picked collage of light that I've somehow not lost—deep in the soup of wedding plans, my future wife and I couldn't bear any more talk of cutlery, calligraphy, and photographer rates and so packed up some snacks, a bottle of Old Crow, and our madcap heeler mutt and on a lark drove out to a ranch where we sat in silence, watching the sky grow dark. Which may seem like a moment not worth plucking from the past's sea, except that our breath grew stale from the bourbon and garlic cheese, and the dog bounded after her soggy tennis ball through the thick grasses again and again as our earth turned and made the sun disappear and although there was hardly any view through the thick cluster of trees and this was just another ordinary day turning to twilight before becoming night once more, I'm telling you, you should have seen it.

↜

I've seen computer-generated flyover videos of ancient Rome where the viewer plunges through the clouds, soars over Tiber Island, then flies through the streets, passing never-rippling cobalt pools and temples of dazzling white. For me, even if some of the buildings are recognizable or the video superimposes its re-creations with shots of what can be seen today, there remains a fundamental disconnect from the past. I just can't seem to make the leap between those summoned-up pristine places and the ruins that I've visited.

Part of the problem with the CGI re-creations is the conspicuous absence of humans. We float past frescoes, red-tiled roofs, whole forests of marble columns, but there's never a brick so much as scuffed

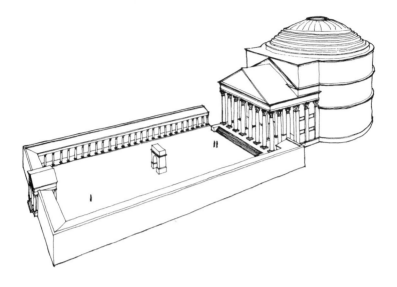

or a torch-smutched wall. It's as if, in a forgotten chapter of history, the Romans couldn't bear the gleam of the immaculate marble world they had made, and so fled for the hills, begging for both forgiveness and beds from the hill-dwelling Etruscans. Whenever the videos do depict a few toga-wearing stragglers, they're never littering rinds of sucked-dry melons or dry-humping against a brick arch. They're more ornament than human, more for scale than veracity, and even when depicted midstride, seem to be processing nowhere at all.

When we inevitably glide toward the Pantheon, there's a jolt in seeing the building as it might have been. A long-gone paved fore-court sprawls several blocks north—its sheer white stone typically garnished with a few black-speck Romans—and restored statues inside cast digital shadows in every niche. And there's the dome as we believe it once was: its coffers painted blue and each one studded with a bronze rosette, their perfect rows aligned like buttons on a shirt.

When it comes to the Pantheon in these computerized worlds,

it's not, of course, that I don't recognize the building, but rather that its immaculate space seems like a sparse, uninviting void. Give me the throngs, the flubbed restorations, the riddle of a wall's palimpsest, that tourist in a "Ciao Pisa!" tank top hollering for Ethan, for Christ's sake, to simmer down. Instead of each of its niches occupied by muscular, marble statues, give me the empty space that reminds us of how we allowed some of the gods to be lost, or stolen, or hammered to bits and taken to kilns where they were melted down and used to strengthen the cement that was needed to construct more buildings that would hold altogether different gods.

Not the exquisite before the ruin comes, but the all-the-more-exquisite almost-ruined.

～

"Because the sky-ground relationship is central to the work," Walter De Maria once wrote, "viewing *The Lightning Field* from the air is of no value."

Since I will never walk across the exterior of the Pantheon's roof and peer down through the oculus—a fact that will never change no matter how much I buck against it—I wish I could be as glib about the thought of looking down into the interior below. Instead, the tantalizing prospect haunts me.

During the heyday of the Grand Tour, when the Pantheon was an essential stop on the Italian itinerary, visitors regularly strolled across the outside of the dome, then clawed their way to the edge of the oculus for a scrotum-tightening peek through that giant eye. Nowadays, however, no one gets to the roof. Whether you blame it on conservation efforts, a newly litigious populace, or the heightened security of our post-9/11 world, unless you're one of those petal-flinging firefighters during Pentecost, you're SOL and, like the rest of us, the only way that you'll be seeing heaven's dome is by craning back your neck.

I've tried to cobble together what the experience of ascending the dome might be like, but with little success. I've been told that the journey would start on one of the many stairwells that honeycomb the building's walls. But rather than clarifying the nature of the Pantheon's concealed interior, these images of the space confuse

and disorient even more. It's as if the ascent might be experienced but never explained.

In some of the photos, Escher-like stairs and passageways seem to defy both gravity and logic. Often, it's impossible to discern the vantage point or what the photograph captures. Some of the hallways don't look as if they would allow any adult-sized person to pass, and affixed to many of the ancient brick arches are anachronistic emergency spotlights and metal shafts housing the building's wiring.

Somewhere—it's hard to understand where—the cramped brick passageways lead to a door that leads to a little walkway and then the dome's lead-covered roof. After all that weaving and ducking and curving through space—presto!—there you are.

The dome used to be covered with panels of gleaming bronze, but that material was looted long ago. The roof now is a kind of slate-gray splotched with white streaks. In terms of sheer aesthetics, it's a bit like looking at, say, the roof of a sewage treatment plant or some humdrum soda-bottling factory.

From the close-ups on the exterior that I've seen, it appears as if the walk up to the oculus would be a fairly easy ascent. There's even a stair-step structure built into the dome's exterior that follows its curve. Yet when I contacted someone who had had the wild good fortune to access the roof decades back, he described that short walk as a straining and vertiginous affair, "a bit like rock climbing up a slope on a hike in the Appalachians."

He also told me that once those exterior stairs ended, the journey felt utterly precarious, and he needed to creep forward toward the oculus on his stomach. Far from some romanticized act of supplication, this was due to the fact that the difference in temperature between the building's cool interior and the sun-warmed roof might potentially create downdrafts that could literally suck visitors through the opening.

And what can one see through the oculus?

On that front, things also remain wholly unclear, which perhaps is appropriate. If the dome was designed to mimic the heavens, a walk across its surface entails a journey across the backside of the gods' celestial home, and, by extension, trying to gaze through that opening must be something like attempting to see through the eyes of the divine.

One visitor wrote that, as he looked below, he saw only darkness punctuated with short bursts of light from the tourists' flashbulbs. "It was like flying," one insisted, "nothing below, and the enormous perfect space breaking away." Another claimed—which of these accounts snares the best metaphor for a god's view?—that he could definitely discern crowds weaving through the space: "I remember looking down at all the tiny people and being keenly aware of how few looked up. Here were a whole crew of bobbing heads ringing the oculus, many of us waving, and no one noticed."

In a photograph that I've seen, none of the visitors to the roof are looking through the oculus at all. One man reclines, seemingly either quite comfortable in this realm not intended for humans or perhaps even a little bored. Some kneel at the edge, keeping their backs to the space, while others point emphatically elsewhere, guiding the gaze of others across the cityscape, looking at who knows what.

⌒

After the planes struck, a storm of debris tumbled down and spread through the streets and steel and glass were replaced with smoke, followed by vacant space. Months went by and nothing filled that span of New York sky until two artists worked to commemorate what was lost with two side-by-side rays of light. These beams in fact were made by nearly a hundred searchlights arranged into two groups and rigged with 7,000-watt xenon bulbs that shone for miles straight up through the night. Close to the skyline, and seen from a distance, the light was so strong as to appear tangible. Yet we all

knew, of course, that there was nothing there to touch, and could see
how those two shafts rose high above the earth, gradually becoming
blue-twinged streaks that blurred into a single luminous thing that
faded, then disappeared.

What is my veering about? Why rummage the past while piling
on *ands*? Why flit from the actual into some metaphor, from the now
to antiquity again?

Part of it is that I don't know how to know without swerves and
accruing proximities and allowing shadows to be cast. Part of it is
that these words are less about any one place than the broad-stroke
need to respond to void and light and what remains after ruin sweeps
through.

Thus I am standing outside again in the Ohio night as a kid,
aiming my flashlight straight up into the star-clustered sky. I flick the
beam on and off in meaningless rhythms, shooting blast upon blast
of fragments of light, imagining my clipped beams soaring off into
blackness, cruising the cosmos, bound to strike something decades on.

And I am thinking again about the Portuguese word *saudade*—
meaning an absence so real that it's become a presence—which was
written to me long ago on a postcard splotched with rain that rendered it nearly illegible and caused me to misread it as *somebody*. Even
after I discovered my mistake, the word careened back and forth,
signifying both absence and a presence until I could no longer tell
one from the other, and even though loss had nothing to do with this,
the card trembled in my hand.

And again I'm looking at footage of those thousands of migrat-
ing birds—whole flocks of warblers, grosbeaks, thrushes, orioles, and
yellowthroats—who were drawn off course by that memorial's beams
and became trapped in those shafts of light. Even as they circle that
empty, luminous space, I'm wishing I would stay put. Even this once,

I want to watch—without turn or trope—and by seeing know how to respond.

⌒

"Here's a bit of description, for what it's worth," Elizabeth Bishop wrote in a letter to Robert Lowell as a means of introducing her poem "The End of March." "It started out as a sort of joke thank-you note," she confessed.

In its opening stanzas, the poem pretends to be a kind of casual depiction of a blustery walk along a beach, with the speaker's eye flitting over whatever happens to be a part of the shore scene. There are a few seabirds scattered in the sky, an icy offshore wind (it's far from an ideal day for a stroll), a sea the color of mutton-fat jade, sand inscribed with lion-size dog prints.

Despite the precision with which these individual details are rendered, the landscape remains sparse and removed: "Everything was withdrawn as far as possible," she writes, "indrawn." Her brisk beach walk doesn't build toward a final insight or meaning but rather comes to an end when she happens to see a scribble of wave-tossed string: "lengths and lengths, endless, of wet white string, / looping up to the tide-line, down to the water, / over and over."

Despite the inclusion of so many stumbled-upon details, it turns out there's been a tacit goal afoot all along:

> I wanted to get as far as my proto-dream-house,
> my crypto-dream-house, that crooked box
> set up on pilings, shingled green,
> a sort of artichoke of a house, but greener
> (boiled with bicarbonate of soda?),
> protected from spring tides by a palisade
> of—are they railroad ties?
> (Many things about this place are dubious.)

Even if she doesn't reach the building on her journey, she can still summon its fragments, ask questions, admit her lapses, understand that it's as much a construction of actual pilings, shingles, and who-knows-what as whatever's concocted in her mind.

Even without ever arriving there, it can remain a place to measure all journeys by. It can be both a secret and a beacon.

〜

I've strolled through a few facts and theories about the Pantheon that have snared my mind and eye, but in the end what's left may also amount to only loop upon loop of snarled, tossed-about stuff. I'll take it. Instead of the lumbering weight of without-doubt facts, grant me shape-shifting churning, crest and trough, the on-the-move cast-out line.

Or let me say it like this: to build the Pantheon's dome, the ancient builders made use of more than five thousand tons of concrete. The walls are twenty feet thick at the base of the dome, but that width gradually narrows to the mere four feet of concrete that ring its oculus. To avoid the dome collapsing under its own weight, they mixed-in porous volcanic rock that lightened the material at the apex of the dome.

All of this we know. But somewhere in there we also guess, or choose to believe, that Apollodorus once quipped to Hadrian, "Be off, and draw your pumpkins," thus insolently sending the emperor away to doodle his scalloped rib-vaulted domes for that villa at Tivoli years before any work on the Pantheon. No matter how many indisputables we crank out, we'll never know much more about the journey from those early prep-work sketches of squash-like shapes to the Pantheon's immense, freestanding, still-standing dome. More importantly, there's poetry in all our guesswork.

There's the forest-of-timbers theory, consisting of a wilderness of wood planks extending from the earth to the heavens to come. There's a centering frame radiating scaffolds and tiers, and there's spot-lagging and siege engines, perhaps coffer molds and a hinged ring of struts. I never thought I would hear a sonic texture as seductive as "scrub oak" until I encountered "the hammer-beam of Viollet-le-Duc."

Last—and a personal favorite—is the piling-up-earth-into-a-rounded-shape, pouring-concrete, waiting-until-it-hardens, then-digging-the-dirt-until-only-a-dome-and-void-remains theory. In order to ensure that such a mass of earth was efficiently removed, the earth that filled and held the dome's form was strewn with gold coins. Or so the legend goes. The volunteer workers could keep whatever coins they found, it seems, which then resulted in 24/7 dirt-shoveling sprees. Although there's nothing in history or architecture to credit this idea—when is form ever that easy? do we ever know exactly where we'll strike gold?—I once heard a Pantheon tour guide describing the earth-into-void process as authentic fact to a group of tourists, all of whom were nodding with relish.

≈

Divine light, Dante tells us, "cannot be set forth in words," although, of course, he tries. Even as he insists that words will always fail to describe what it's like to ascend from the earth into Paradise and be swaddled in celestial blaze, the light, he tells us, nonetheless, seemed like an iron pulled gleaming from the fire, like day added to day. And when he gazes upon Beatrice gazing upon that glow—for what first holds the poet rapt is not a head-on looking—he feels himself forever transformed, just like that moment, he tells us, when Glaucus became a god.

What a wild arc one must tack at times in order to stay on course.

To paraphrase where the poet has just set sail: the act of looking upon the woman whom he loves looking upon heavenly light is like the story of a Greek fisherman who crammed some nearby grassy stuff into the gaping mouths of a few dead fish—what prompted this, who knows?—and watched their gills begin heaving yet again and thought *why not* before chomping down on a few fistfuls of the herb, which, it turned out, were somehow magic or blessed, and he felt his heart skitter and slam in his chest and could not resist the newly beckoning sea and even though he knew at once that now he would never die, he wasn't thinking about the forever-life stretching before him or the way his feet had become rubbery fins, but rather he felt some kind of departure deep in his soul and as he splashed out across the waves, it seemed as if the only words he knew were O *earth, farewell.*

≈

Long ago, the Pantheon's roof offered no glimpse of the sky above and no light roamed below. At least so some believed. Its dome had been built as a sealed-shut slab of concrete, capped for some reason by an enormous stone pinecone.

Some nights, they could hear a hissing from behind the doors, an occasional demonic chuckle. At times, what remained of the Roman statues wobbled or scooched as if cocooning something inside.

Basta, the pope at last decreed, and begged permission from the Byzantine emperor to consecrate the building in the name of the one true god. Thus either wielding nothing but a wooden cross or twenty-eight cartloads of martyrs' bones—depending which version you want to believe—he stormed the Pantheon alone, or perhaps with an army of priests, and the dervishing demons, desperate to exit, screeched and rammed the dome, apparently ripping a perfect hole in its roof and hurling the pinecone through miles of air, where it landed in a courtyard at the Vatican and can be seen to this day.

Faced with our slew of immensities, a sky we can't see until something is rent, we give air to another *once-upon-a-time*, seize on something within reach.

When my grandfather died, part of his funeral was given over to Masonic rites. At some point during the ceremony, two men from the Brotherhood whom I had never seen before walked to the casket and stood looming over his body. For what seemed like a long time, they gazed at us in silence. One held what looked like a square of cloth, the other grasped a branch of pine. Light poured in from the funeral parlor windows, cars mopped slush on the road.

At last one of them spoke. He said something solemn and scripted about the Masons—I forget what—then held aloft his tasseled cloth and, before laying it on my grandfather's chest, announced that the lambskin apron was more ancient than the Roman eagle or Golden Fleece. The other man held up a small branch of pine. "This Ever-

green," he said, holding the branch aloft, "represents eternal life," and then placed it somewhere out of sight in the casket.

⌒

In one medieval illustration of the Tower of Babel story, the entire human workforce is distilled to just nine men. Four workers chisel rocks below; one is caught on the tower's threshold, shouldering a basket loaded with stones; and three are perched in the crenellated peak, hoisting up stones using tongs, pulleys, and buckets. One of the workers has paused in order to gaze up at God's scowling face already jabbing down through the azure's upper edge.

This version of the story—featuring a god who has become, it seems, a bit like a crabby, geriatric neighbor, shaking his fist at those who have trespassed across a few feet of his infinite Elysian field—is consistent with what I learned about that tower in Sunday school as a child. The shorthand: in our insolence we believed that we might rise until we reached heaven, but a trigger-happy God offered a proper-order, know-your-place smackdown blow, thus scattering us across the earth and forever scrambling our words, ensuring that we'd never again stack stones in that manner.

But look again: the text of Genesis suggests a less didactic tale.

"Behold," God says, observing our work, "the people is one, and they have all one language; and this they begin to do: and now nothing will be restrained from them, which they have imagined to do."

Consider this story beyond its Kipling-esque "Just So" framework ("And that's why some call the oxen *niu* and some call them *ng'ombe*"). Instead of a territorial god, imagine a benevolent deity who saw what we were trying to build and wanted to save us from omniscience and blind efficiency and the path of *Noi tireremo diritto* that tempts our unsteady hearts. Who knew our salvation lay in obfuscation, in not knowing, in the dazzling out-of-reach.

"Many things about this place are dubious," Elizabeth Bishop wrote in "The End of March," whereby begins our flubbed guesswork, all our many baffling tongues.

Babel, from *balal*, meaning "to jumble," which affords the wonder we need to thrive.

The Pantheon, of course, could not have been constructed without meticulous engineering—each hidden buttress, the mathematical means of lightening its concrete's weight, stone mortared precisely to stone. But now that building's unfathomable scale seems less about stressing what can be ascertained than about underscoring all we don't know.

Here is a disc of sky, a beam of light that arrives, then disappears. Here are bricks stacked and arranged whose real purpose—beautifully—from us will forever be withheld.

⌒

"Inhabit," we say, from the Old French, meaning "to dwell," but we inherit its root from *habere*, meaning "to have, to hold."

I always knew that my stay in Italy would be for a limited window of time, and before I left Rome and returned to New Mexico after living abroad, I hoped to have some means of remembering what it was like to inhabit the Pantheon's space. Or, to put it another way, I wanted somehow to possess it.

Standing beneath the oculus with all the other summer tourists, I photographed the dome's light-glazed coffers once more. I took detail shots of its mottled marble, the green patina of its bronze doors, the pilasters above Raphael's tomb, knowing I'd never be able to document it all, knowing each snapshot in its own way would fail.

I also set out to find a Pantheon souvenir. Or rather, based on a hokey, half-baked theory, to confirm that souvenirs of the building didn't exist because the singular beauty of its structure could not be

replicated. A sentimental notion? Absolutely, but that didn't change the fact that in all the piles of Italian tchotchkes I'd seen—snow globes of the Leaning Tower and the Colosseum, pope lollipops (two euros each, except for John Paul II, which will run you fifty euro cents more), Trevi Fountain pens, *Last Supper* magnets, Vespa bottle-openers, plastic wolf-suckling twins, "Pure-Silk!" boxers designed with the iconic stone pubes of Michelangelo's David—I had never once encountered a miniaturized Pantheon capping a keychain or caught in a swirl of fake snow.

Then, of course, I found one. Actually, I found a whole pile of Pantheons heaped in a wicker basket. Each weighed about a pound and was barely the thing that it was meant to be. Recognizable, yet indiscernible, it was like stumbling upon a photograph of a lover from a time long past: it seemed both familiar and yet entirely different from what in my mind I knew to be true.

Made of something like plaster, the souvenirs resembled the building only in the loosest sense. There was a square-shaped portico lined with a few matchstick-like columns and capped with a crooked triangular roof. And there was the cylindrical shape scored to look as if it were constructed of layers of bricks, misted with some kind of rust-colored, antiquating dye. Across the souvenir's base, stamped in bold capitals that were broken across the middle, I read "PANT HEON." If, for a moment, I considered the correspondence between the building's roof and that word's down-the-middle split, if I was drawn to the way in which that caesura ruptured the Pantheon's all-too-familiar name, I also knew most likely that the two words signified nothing at all.

Is it ever enough, what we grapple after for meaning, for solace, in order to guess and gaze even more?

Without taking a stab at bargaining, I forked over five euros and walked away with one in my hand.

Notes

◡

EPIGRAPH

". . . nubem inusitata et magnitudine et specie," reads Pliny the Younger's Latin description of the sudden apparition towering over Vesuvius. While "size" and "shape" seem to be more or less appropriate renderings into English, translating *inusitata* into "unusual" may not adequately convey Pliny's sense of wonder. "Extraordinary" perhaps comes closer to conjuring the awe he seems to have felt upon seeing that decimating cloud. The epigraph's translation is by John B. Firth.

LEAVING TRINITY:
TEN GROUND ZERO SWERVES

PAGE 10, *the backseat of a Plymouth sedan*   For facts involving the Trinity Site test, I'm deeply indebted to Richard Rhodes's *The Making of the Atomic Bomb*.

PAGE 12, *changes them into an abstraction*   From "Mr. Cogito Reads the Newspaper," Alissa Valles translation.

PAGE 17, *on one of its central architects*   No less revealing, however, is the cavalier response by Paul Tibbets, the pilot of the *Enola Gay*, who reenacted his bombing of Hiroshima for a 1976 Texas air show. Before tens of thousands of spectators, Tibbets flew in a plane named *Fifi* and dropped explosives designed to produce a mushroom-shaped cloud of smoke.

This essay is dedicated to David Wojahn.

HOUSE OF THE VETTII

PAGE 23, *in the Hotel Park Plaza's Meridian Room*   Specific references to Welles's broadcast have been appropriated from the original radio transcript, as reprinted in Howard Koch's *The Panic Broadcast* (New York: Avon Books, 1970).

PAGE 24, *"Bring the torch burning"*   Quotations from Euripides' *Bakkhai* taken from the Reginald Gibbons translation.

PAGE 24, *and you'd earn thirty-five bucks*   "The Citizens of Lawrence, Kansas Get a Glimpse of Armageddon as Performers in ABC's *The Day After*," *People Magazine*, November 21, 1983.

PAGE 26, *In order to train his actors for the moment*   According to Joe Bevilacqua's radio documentary, "We Now Take You to Grover's Mill: The Making of the 'War of the Worlds' Broadcast."

PAGE 29, *"the end of the world?"*   "Radio Listeners in Panic, Taking War Drama as Fact," *New York Times*, October 31, 1938.

PAGE 33, *after the actual bomb was dropped*   Robert Jay Lifton and Greg Mitchell, *Hiroshima in America: A Half Century of Denial* (New York: Harper Perennial, 1996), 374.

PAGE 35, *would you want me to look at the sky*   A paraphrase of Gibbons's translation.

HOUSE OF THE FAUN

PAGE 41, *mosaic discovered at the House of the Faun*   August Mau, *Pompeii: Its Life and Art* (New York: Macmillan, 1902), 293.

PAGE 44, *"Too hot, too hot"*   According to the photographer Nick Ut.

GARDEN OF THE FUGITIVES

PAGE 49, *This time, in the Villa of Diomedes*   Quoted in Eugene Dwyer, *Pompeii's Living Statues: Ancient Roman Lives Stolen from Death* (Ann Arbor: University of Michigan Press, 2010), 12.

PAGE 50, *"memorializing their figures"*   Amedeo Maiuri, "Last Moments of the Pompeiians," *National Geographic*, November 1961, 659.

PAGE 52, *"at the signal of the angel's trumpet"*   Maiuri, "Last Moments," 661.

PAGE 54, *Pockmarks of air bubbles freckling the plaster* Estelle Lazer, *Resurrecting Pompeii* (New York: Routledge, 2009), 254.

PAGE 54, *"The Wreck of the Medusa"* Quoted in Dwyer, *Pompeii's Living Statues*, 10.

PAGE 56, *as easy as flipping a coin* Eugene Dwyer, "From Fragments to Icons: Stages in the Making and Exhibiting of the Casts of Pompeian Victims, 1863–1888," *Interpreting Ceramics* 8 (2005).

PAGE 58, *in a vehicle dogged by armed escorts* Lazer, *Resurrecting Pompeii*, 260.

PAGE 59, *The Dog from Pompei* As opposed to *The Dog from Pompeii*. McCollum's gallery was rightfully emphatic that the town's name in the title of the piece not be misspelled with that extra "i." Such a distinction, though small, insists that the dog cast belongs to the modern Italian city of Pompei, versus the ancient town of Pompeii, further underscoring the distance between the world of antiquity and our experience with those plaster forms.

PAGE 59, *shorthand for something we've already seen* Despite repeat visits to the site, I've never seen the so-called "Pompei dog." However, I once saw its glass case, empty except for a wedge of Styrofoam inscribed with black marker. "On display in Halle," the makeshift sign read in Italian, indicating nothing at all about what artifact normally inhabited the box-shaped vitrine when it wasn't in Germany. Perhaps the squat shape of the case, or the plaster dog's location there among the ruins, is as well known as the plaster form itself. Perhaps the actual canine plaster shape is no longer required in order to serve as signifier.

PAGE 61, *rapiti alla morti* Dwyer, *Pompeii's Living Statues*, vii.

HOUSE OF THE TRAGIC POET

PAGE 64, *The audience, some guessed, looked so enthralled* William Gell, *Pompeiana: The Topography, Edifices and Ornaments of Pompeii, the Result of Excavations since 1819*, 2: 112.

PAGE 64, *By the time new theories were set afloat* The imagined poem here is loosely based on details from Seneca's *Agamemnon*.

PAGE 65, *that her husband must die* Mary Beard, *Pompeii: The Life of a Roman Town* (London: Profile Books, 2010), 82.

PAGE 66, *at last a spade struck his skull*   Details of Shelley's drowning and funeral have been taken from Edward Trelawny's *Recollections of the Last Days of Shelley and Byron*.

PAGE 66, *had paddled off into the surf*   More specifically, Trelawny relates a machismo contest erupting while Shelley's body burned: "'Let us try the strength of these waters that drowned our friends,' said Byron, with his usual audacity. 'How far out do you think they were when their boat sank?'"

PAGE 67, *saucepans, some rope, a few terra-cotta frogs*   Gell, *Pompeiana*, 1:169.

HOUSE OF THE LARGE FOUNTAIN

PAGE 70, *From there, it would have been channeled*   Beard, *Pompeii*, 64.

PAGE 70, *were designed to hold candles*   Wilhelmina F. Jashemski, *The Gardens of Pompeii* (New Rochelle, N.Y.: Caratzas Brothers, 1979), 2: 135.

PAGE 70, *in the years before Pompeii was destroyed*   Jashemski, *The Gardens of Pompeii*, 1: 41.

PAGE 70, *something fairly ghastly*   William Clark, *Pompeii* (London, Charles Knight, 1832), 2:174.

PAGE 73, *painted toward the top of the bricks*   Gell, *Pompeiana*, 2:126.

PAGE 73, *leaves flecked with red flowers still remained*   Jashemski, *Gardens of Pompeii*, 2: 343.

PAGE 74, *water bubbles and ripples night and day*   Paul Manship's Hercules fountain in the courtyard at the American Academy in Rome.

PAGE 76, *"the stony vault of heaven"*   According to Calvert Watkins's *American Heritage Dictionary of Indo-European Roots*.

PAGE 76, *to serve as a backdrop for the life of Jesus*   Production details taken from Marilyn Ann Moss, *Giant: George Stevens, a Life on Film* (Madison: University of Wisconsin Press, 2004), 281.

PAGE 77, *at last fully submerged*   According to the 2001 documentary *He Walks in Beauty: The George Stevens Production "The Greatest Story Ever Told."*

PAGE 77, *"and grumbled like a lion"*   Descriptions of the 1944 eruption of Vesuvius are taken from the personal diaries of members of the 489th Bomb Squadron, available online.

PAGE 82, *the entire island back to the bay* Marvel Team-Up #128 is apparently reviled as one of the worst Spider-Man comic books of all time (one small step up from the disco showdown in "Death Dance of the Hypno-Hustler"). Its premise was so transparently shoddy that the comic's last panel included a text box with a disclaimer, a pointed jab at the writer, and an implicit promise to compensate in the future: "SPECIAL NOTE FROM YE EDITOR! So that's the way that Merry Gerry told it to us, friend! And, quite frankly, we're not sure if WE believe it, either! Why the damage to the Triboro Bridge and Lincoln Tunnel alone would have—well, anyway—NEXT issue, don't miss 'The Coming of INFINITUS' co-starring The Human Torch and Iron Man!"

PAGE 83, *"Who could tell beast from man?"* Quotations from Euripides' *Herakles* taken from the Tom Sleigh translation.

VILLA OF THE MYSTERIES

PAGE 86, *induction into Dionysian rites* See, for example, Joanne Berry, *The Complete Pompeii* (London: Thames & Hudson, 2007), 202.

PAGE 86, *flogging were transparent enough* Beard, *Pompeii*, 132.

PAGE 86, *"whatever you want them to mean"* John R. Clarke, in conversation.

PAGE 86, *striding in and spewing benedictions* "The goddess Aura descends from heaven, her mantle filled by wind," writes Umberto Pappalardo in Donatella Mazzoleni's *Domus: Wall Painting in the Roman House*. "A woman (group C) who seems to have wandered into this divine realm, appears startled, even frightened, either at the sight of the god himself (group D) or by the scenes that follow—the revelation of the phallus (group E) and a demon flagellating a young initiate as a maenad dances (group F)," writes Elaine K. Gazda in her essay "Ancient and Modern Contexts of the Bacchic Murals in the Villa of the Mysteries."

PAGE 88, *enacting its inevitable changes* Details of these excavation and preservation efforts are explored in Bettina Bergmann's "Seeing Women in the Villa of the Mysteries: A Modern Excavation of the Dionystic Murals."

PAGE 95, *"if my eyes had been turned from it"* John D. Sinclair's translation of *Paradiso*.

DEW POINT

PAGE 104, *"A bath when you're born"*   Robert Hass translation.

PAGE 104, *"Dewdrops falling"*   David Lanoue translation.

PAGE 106, *"and yet" becomes "although"*   Other renderings in English include:

"The world of dew— / A world of dew it is indeed, / And yet, and yet . . . "
"This world of dew / is only the world of dew / and yet . . . oh and yet"
"The world is dew— / The world is dew— / And yet, and yet"
"This world of dew / is only a world of dew— / and yet"
"A world of dew / it is indeed, / And yet, and yet . . . "
"The world of dew / is only the world of dew / and yet."
"The world of dew is, yes, / a world of dew, / but even so"

PAGE 112, *"Disappears like dew"*   Mary Elizabeth Berry translation.

PAGE 112, *"a phantom, or a dream"*   Alex Johnson translation.

PAGE 115, *The wall with the window*   These examples of *giornata* are borrowed from Umberto Baldini and Ornella Casazza's *The Brancacci Chapel* (New York: Abrams, 1992).

PAGE 115, *"Worth a look"*   David Lanoue translation.

PAGE 115, *"Even the thorn bush"*   David Lanoue translation.

PAGE 117, *"clutched her cold body and wailed"*   Issa Kobayashi and Sam Hamill, *The Spring of My Life and Selected Haiku* (Boston: Shambhala, 1997), 63.

PAGE 117, *"a hard promise to keep, Paul"*   William Granger Ryan translation.

MONKEY MIND:

A MEDITATIVE PATH TO PERFECTION

PAGE 125, *"a whole movie in a single frame?"*   www.sugimotohiroshi.com

PAGE 125, *murals of Grecian urns*   Or a flagpole, an organ, tassels, and pleats. Eight corkscrewing Solomonic columns, statues of winged, nearly naked, torch-bearing women, three different breeds of painted faux stars.

PAGE 126, *"the truth and insight of things"*   Nancy G. Hume, *Japanese Aesthetics and Culture: A Reader* (Albany: SUNY Press, 1995), 126.

PAGE 126, *"My needle is slow to settle"*   All quotations by Thoreau taken from his essay "Walking."

PAGE 127, *headlights skating Highway 67* For many viewers, car headlights coupled with the eagerness of spectators to experience something inexplicable sufficiently account for this Marfa phenomenon. That said, the viewing station constructed on Highway 90 remains a popular tourist destination, and the Mystery Lights have been written about in publications ranging from the *Wall Street Journal* to the anecdote-packed paperback *The Marfa Lights, Being a Collection of First-Hand Accounts by People Who Have Seen the Lights Close-Up or in Unusual Circumstances, and Related Material.* While additional explanations have been posited, I'll happily sidestep swamp gas and UFOs for the bioluminescent barn owl theory.

AGAINST DESIRE

PAGE 132, *"our new Cheddar Explosion is dynamite"* Kraft also apparently sponsored a video companion piece to their marketing campaign that climaxed with a CGI mushroom cloud blast of molten cheese.

NO FULLER ON EARTH

PAGE 146, *"I choose to cut my materials by hand"* All quotations by Kate Carr taken from the artist's website, www.katecarrart.com.

PAGE 147, *Goethe, on the other hand* Information about Raphael's last painting taken from *A Masterpiece Close-Up: The Transfiguration by Raphael* (Vatican City: Libreria Editrice Vaticana, 1979).

PAGE 151, *"gleams in all its power"*   Stephen Mitchell translation. This essay is dedicated to Kate Carr and Jenny George.

TOWARD SOME BLOSSOMS MORE OR LESS

PAGE 155, *"For the enjoyment of the cherry blossoms"*   Hari Prasad Shastri, "O Hanami: Flower Viewing," in *Seeing God Everywhere*, ed. Barry McDonald (Bloomington, Ind.: World Wisdom, 2003), 134.

PAGE 155, *"More than ever I want to see"*   *The Essential Haiku: Versions of Bashō, Buson, and Issa*, trans. Robert Hass (New York: Ecco, 1994), 37.

PAGE 155, *"I do not like this thing of being silent"*   Dwight Young and Margaret Johnson, eds., *Dear First Lady: Letters to the White House* (Washington, D.C.: National Geographic, 2008), 77.

PAGE 156, *"Occasions do arise"*   "Topics of the Times: Wounding to Japanese Sensibility," *New York Times*, January 31, 1910. Or this, from the February 1 *Washington Post* editorial "Another Cherry Tree Lie": "When will the representatives of the United States government ever learn that the truth should be used sparingly in commercial affairs?"

PAGE 156, *"The idea," the article concluded*   "Mrs. Taft Plants a Tree," *Washington Post*, March 28, 1912.

PAGE 156, *"form masses, or continuous lines of bright color"*   Lewis L. Gould, *Helen Taft: Our Musical First Lady* (Lawrence: University Press of Kansas, 2010), 46.

PAGE 156, *"of music, gayety, and athletics"*   Ann McClellan, *The Cherry Blossom Festival: Sakura Celebration* (Boston: Bunker Hill, 2005), 31.

PAGE 156, *"umbrageous beauty"*   "Bring On the Cherry Trees!" *Washington Post*, August 29, 1909: E4.

PAGE 157, *Some scholars suggest the poem references Hitokotonushi*   *Bashō's Journey: The Literary Prose of Matsuo Bashō*, trans. David Landis Barnhill (Albany: SUNY Press, 2005), 152. Barnhill's translation of the same poem reads: "All the more I'd like to see it / with dawn coming to the blossoms: / the face of the god."

PAGE 158, *while anchored in the Harbor of Makang*   Michael E. Ruane, "D.C.'s

Cherry Blossoms and the Sad Story of Japanese Family," *Washington Post*, March 26, 2010.

PAGE 159, *"full of the story of our sorrow?"* Robert Fitzgerald translation.

PAGE 159, *"there is something"* Barnhill, *Bashō's Journey*, 29.

PAGE 160, *"forced into flowering artificially"* "Japan's Debt to US Heavy, Says Chinda," *New York Times*, March 17, 1912.

PAGE 160, *"War has had its day," he declared* Ruane, "D.C.'s Cherry Blossoms," B1.

PAGE 161, *in order to avoid capture* Helen Craig McCullough, *The Tale of the Heike* (Stanford, Calif.: Stanford University Press, 1988), 378.

PAGE 162, *Turns Again to Look and See* David Fairchild, *The World Was My Garden* (New York: Charles Scribner's Sons, 1938), 411.

PAGE 162, *"they bring to mind— / cherry blossoms!"* Robert Aitken, *A Zen Wave: Bashō's Haiku and Zen* (Washington, D.C.: Shoemaker and Hoard, 2003), 102. Such as, for instance, this haiku by Issa: "The cherry tree / that made blossom clouds / becomes charcoal" (David Lanoue translation).

PAGE 164, *"the last petal has fluttered to the earth"* "8,000 Brave Cold to Cheer Coronation of Cherry Queen," *Washington Post*, April 14, 1940.

PAGE 164, *on one severed trunk* "Japan's Mark Is Taboo," *Washington Post*, December 11, 1941.

PAGE 165, *"from root to twig top"* "Those Cherry Trees Aren't Jap after All," *Washington Post*, April 5, 1942.

PAGE 169, *"and I could only close my mouth":* Barnhill, *Bashō's Journey, 39.*

PAGE 169, *"from all thoughts and ideas"* Hagoromo Society of Kamikaze Divine Thunderbolt Corps Survivors, *The Cherry Blossom Squadrons: Born to Die* (Los Angeles: Ohara Publications, 1973), 28.

PAGE 169, *for Blossom Festival Heads* *Washington Post*, March 29, 1947.

ALMOST A FULL YEAR OF STONE, LIGHT, AND SKY

PAGE 174, *and theon, meaning "of the gods"* Mark Wilson Jones, *Principles of Roman Architecture* (New Haven, Conn.: Yale University Press, 2009), 179.

PAGE 175, *in which all of the gods reside*   Jones, *Principles*, 179.

PAGE 175, *like that of a prototypical house*   An idea I first encountered in Pietro Pucci's entry on the Pantheon in the *City Secrets: Rome* guidebook.

PAGE 180, *at his own wound*   Adrian Goldsworthy, *Caesar: Life of a Colossus* (New Haven, Conn.: Yale University Press, 2008), 469.

PAGE 182, *"It was not just blue"*   George McKenna, *The Puritan Origins of American Patriotism* (New Haven, Conn.: Yale University Press, 2009), 350.

PAGE 182, *"A late-summer sky"*   Robert Mann, *Forensic Detective: How I Cracked the World's Toughest Cases* (New York: Ballantine Books), 166. I'm indebted here to *New York Magazine*'s online "Encyclopedia of 9/11," which gathers several of these descriptions under the heading "Blue."

PAGE 184, *"the visible image of our universe"*   From *Letters of Percy Bysshe Shelley*.

PAGE 184, *different dwelling spaces for the gods*   Jones, *Principles*, 183.

PAGE 185, *bound by nothing at all*   Nancy Thomson de Grummond, *Etruscan Myth, Sacred History, and Legend* (Philadelphia: University of Pennsylvania Museum of Archaeology and Anthropology, 2006), 50.

PAGE 187, *when exposed to its light and scale*   Jones, *Principles*, 199.

PAGE 190, *built by the Emperor Hadrian*   William L. MacDonald, *The Pantheon: Design, Meaning, and Progeny* (Cambridge, Mass.: Harvard University Press, 2002), 13.

PAGE 197, *not needing to guess about anything*   Much later, however, I did find myself guessing what it would have been like to tour the Pantheon by boat after too much rain in the seventeenth century resulted in a complete flood of the building.

PAGE 197, *"Nothing remained of the former structure"*   Marguerite Yourcenar, *Memoirs of Hadrian* (New York: Farrar, Straus and Giroux, 2005), 167.

PAGE 198, *builders in lieu of his own*   Thomas Opper, *Hadrian: Empire and Conflict* (Cambridge, Mass.: Harvard University Press, 2008), 239.

PAGE 201, *would have come from Attica*   Opper, *Hadrian*, 116.

PAGE 202, *cannot be contemplated without horror*   From Walter Benjamin's "Theses on the Philosophy of History."

PAGE 202, *before it reached its destination*   Borden Painter, *Mussolini's Rome: Rebuilding the Eternal City* (New York: Palgrave Macmillan, 2007), 41.

PAGE 205, *just below the building's midway point*   Tod A. Marder, "Bernini and

Alexander VII: Criticism and Praise of the Pantheon in the Seventeenth Century," *Art Bulletin* 71 (December 1989): 629.

PAGE 205, *for a single raucous night*   Information about Posi's restorations explained in *An Account of the Alterations Made in the Pantheon at Rome in an Extract of a Letter from Rome to Thomas Hollis* (published by the Royal Society).

PAGE 206, *"the middle is stunning," Kiefer claimed*   As quoted in *Spiegel Online International*, October 31, 2011.

PAGE 207, *killing four students and wounding nine others*   Philip Caputo, *13 Seconds: A Look Back at the Kent State Shootings* (New York: Chamberlain Bros., 2005), 71.

PAGE 208, *would have fully sealed the building's oculus*   Tod A. Marder, *Bernini and the Art of Architecture* (New York: Abbeville Press, 1998), 232.

PAGE 208, *"in front of the left column"*   Tod A. Marder, "Alexander VII, Bernini, and the Urban Setting of the Pantheon in the Seventeenth Century," *Journal of the Society of Architectural Historians* 50 (September 1991): 276.

PAGE 216, *"on a hike in the Appalachians"*   Quotes about climbing the Pantheon taken from email correspondence with Ron Musto, and the Facebook comments of Bunny Harvey and Roy W. Lewis.

PAGE 216, *Another claimed—which of these accounts snares*   In the only photograph I've seen from the vantage point of the oculus, all the components of the building are reduced to geometric abstraction. But would the image carry any whiff of the sublime for the viewer who had never entered the Pantheon's doors? What response could we have to the coffer's vague recessions, the marble floor's pattern of circles and squares, without having first gazed up?

PAGE 218, *straight up through the night*   The Municipal Art Society of New York website.

PAGE 219, *trapped in those shafts of light*   See Andrew Farnsworth's Tribute in Light Memorial bird-watching checklist online at ebird.org.

PAGE 219, *"a sort of joke thank-you note," she confessed*   From *Words in Air: The Complete Correspondence between Elizabeth Bishop and Robert Lowell*, ed. Thomas Travisano and Saskia Hamilton (New York: Farrar, Straus and Giroux, 2008), 667.

PAGE 221, *his scalloped rib-vaulted domes*   Jones, *Principles*, 23.

PAGE 221, *"the hammer-beam of Viollet-le-Duc"*   These theories compiled from Rabun Taylor, *Roman Builders: A Study in Architectural Process* (Cambridge: Cambridge University Press, 2003).

PAGE 222, *although, of course, he tries*   John D. Sinclair's translation of *Paradiso*.

PAGE 222, *only words he knew were* O earth, farewell   Paraphrased from David R. Slavitt's translation of Ovid.

Image Sources

⤲

PAGE 5 Norman Mauskopf, *Trinity Site, Jornada del Muerto, New Mexico, 2005,* © Norman Mauskopf.

PAGE 6 Harold Edgerton, "Milk Drop Coronet (series)," © 2010 MIT. Courtesy of MIT Museum.

PAGE 8 Norman Mauskopf, *Trinity Site, Jornada del Muerto, New Mexico, 2005,* © Norman Mauskopf.

PAGE 10 Manhattan Project patch (author's photograph).

PAGE 13 Jan W. Faul, McDonald Ranch Trinity Assembly Room, © 1998 Jan W. Faul, worldwar2memories.com/2015.

PAGE 14 Oppenheimer and Groves, Ground Zero, 1945 (U.S. Department of Energy).

PAGE 19 Aerial view of the aftermath of the first atomic explosion at Trinity Test Site, New Mexico, July 16, 1945 (U.S. Department of Energy).

PAGE 27 The *Hindenburg* as she crashed to the ground in 1937 after catching fire, Lakehurst Air Station, N.J. (Times Wide World / The New York Times / Redux).

PAGE 29 Publicity still, *The Day After,* © Photographer / American Broadcasting Companies, Inc.

PAGE 30 Pentheus being torn by maenads. Roman fresco from the northern wall of the triclinium in the Casa dei Vettii (VI 15,1) in

Pompeii. © User: Wolfgang Rieger / Wikimedia Commons / CC-BY-SA-3.0 & GFDL.

PAGE 32 Video still, Operation Upshot-Knothole, 1953 (U.S. Department of Energy).

PAGE 33 Video still, the remains of Kansas City / Hiroshima, *The Day After.*

PAGE 37 Satyr statue replica, House of the Faun, Pompeii (author's photograph).

PAGE 39 House of the Faun, "The tetrastyle atrium after it was damaged," from Emilio Lavagnino's *Fifty War-Damaged Monuments of Italy.*

PAGE 41 Detail of Pompeii mosaic depicting Dionysus riding beast (author's photograph).

PAGE 44 Berthold Werner, Naples, National Archaeological Museum, © Berthold Werner / Wikimedia Commons / CC-BY-SA-3.0 & GFDL.

PAGE 46 Detail of fresco depicting sacrifice of Iphigenia (author's photograph).

PAGE 52 Fiorelli completing a plaster body cast, from *Pompeii: The Guide to the Archeological Site* (courtesy Adriano Spano).

PAGE 53 Plaster body cast near Porta Nocera, Pompeii (author's photograph).

PAGE 55 Rachel Whiteread, *Untitled (Torso)*, © 1991 Rachel Whiteread (courtesy of the artist, Luhring Augustine, New York, Lorcan O'Neill, Rome, and Gagosian Gallery).

PAGE 60 Allan McCollum, *The Dog from Pompei*, 1991. Cast glass-fiber-reinforced Hydrocal. Approximately 21 x 21 x 21 inches each. Replicas made from a mold taken from the famous original "chained dog" plaster cast of a dog smothered in ash from the explosion of Mount Vesuvius, in ancient Pompeii, in 79 A.D. Produced in collaboration with the Museo Vesuviano and the Pompei Tourist Board, Pompei, Italy, and Studio Trisorio, Naples, Italy. Installation: Sprengel Museum, Hanover, Germany, 1995 (courtesy of the artist and Petzel, New York).

PAGE 66 Louis Édouard Fournier, *The Funeral of Shelley*, Google Art Project, Wikimedia Commons / CC-BY-SA-3.0 & GFDL.

PAGE 67 House of the Tragic Poet, Pompeii.

PAGE 71 Hercules stone mask, House of the Large Fountain, Pompeii (author's photograph).

PAGE 72 Pompeii Porta Nola, © Jackie and Bob Dunn, www .pompeiiinpictures.com.

PAGE 74 Wall and faded fresco at House of the Large Fountain, Pompeii (author's photograph).

PAGE 75 *Heracliscus Fountain*, photograph by Paul Manship (American Academy in Rome Photographic Archive).

PAGE 78 North American B-25s fly past Mount Vesuvius during an eruption (U.S. Air Force).

PAGE 80 Cyrus Bouton Donovan, *The Story Rocks*.

PAGE 82 Hercules restoring Manhattan, *Marvel Team Up, Volume 1, No. 28*, © MARVEL.

PAGE 87 Fresco detail, Villa of the Mysteries, Pompeii (author's photograph).

PAGE 88 William Lamson, *Irving Pointing to God*, 2003 (courtesy William Lamson).

PAGE 90 Tetrastyle atrium at the Villa of the Mysteries, Pompeii, © User: Mosborne01 / Wikimedia Commons / CC-BY-SA-3.0 & GFDL.

PAGE 93 Fresco detail, Villa of the Mysteries, Pompeii (author's photograph).

PAGE 95 Richard Barnes, AAR Fellow, 2006, *Starlings over Rome, Murmur #1*, 2005.

PAGE 97 Pointing tourists, Villa of the Mysteries, Pompeii (author's photograph).

PAGE 104 Masaccio, detail from *The Expulsion from the Garden of Eden*, Brancacci Chapel, Florence, Wikimedia Commons / CC-BY-SA-3.0 & GFDL.

PAGE 105 Masaccio, detail from *The Holy Trinity*, Church of Santa Maria Novella, Florence, User: Rufus46 / Wikimedia Commons / CC-BY-SA-3.0 & GFDL.

PAGE 109 Masolino da Panicale, detail from *The Temptation of Adam and Eve*, Brancacci Chapel, Florence, Wikimedia Commons / CC-BY-SA-3.0 & GFDL.

PAGE 116 Masaccio, detail from *The Tribute Money*, Brancacci Chapel, Florence, from Baldini and Casazza's, *The Brancacci Chapel* (New York: Abrams, 1992).

PAGE 119 Masaccio, detail from *The Raising of the Son of Theophilus and St. Peter Enthroned*, Brancacci Chapel, Florence, Wikimedia Commons / CC-BY-SA-3.0 & GFDL.

PAGE 138 Home video still (author's collection).

PAGE 143 Kate Carr, *Muslin Box 3*, unbleached muslin, found box, 2007, © Kate Carr.

PAGE 145 Kate Carr, *Through*, Baltic birch plywood, wool felt, 2012, © Kate Carr.

PAGE 150 Kate Carr, *Pillow Bust*, cast plaster, 2006, © Kate Carr.

PAGE 153 Kate Carr, detail of *Muslin Coil*, muslin, 2010, © Kate Carr.

PAGE 157 The 1910 burning of the first shipment of Japanese cherry trees (U.S. National Arboretum).

PAGE 162 Photographers shooting cherry blossoms, Washington, D.C., April 7, 1922 (Library of Congress).

PAGE 163 Diana Pabst Parsell, Washington, D.C., cherry tree plaque, 2012 © Diana Pabst Parsell.

PAGE 165 The Ohka cherry blossom insignia on the Ohka 2 kamikaze plane, © SWNS.

PAGE 167 Shunkichi Kikuchi, charred camphor tree standing in the ruins, © Harumi Tago.

PAGE 168 Daniel Regner, Cherry blossom balloons, National Cherry Blossom Festival Parade, © Daniel Regner.

PAGE 174 West view, upper part of Chambersystem (Bern Digital Pantheon Project).

PAGE 176 Cyrus Bouton Donovan, winter house (author's collection).

PAGE 181 Walter De Maria, *The Lightning Field*, 1977, long-term installation, western New Mexico. © The Estate of Walter De Maria. Courtesy Dia Art Foundation, New York. Photo: John Cliett.

PAGE 183 Lyle Owerko, untitled 9/11 photograph, courtesy of Lyle Owerko.

PAGE 185 Southeast side dome inside rotunda (Bern Digital Pantheon Project).

PAGE 186 Section of the cupola with plaster knocked off (American Academy in Rome Photographic Archive).

PAGE 191 Tobias Kirchway, Pantheon, light on attic zone.

PAGE 192 Pantheon oculus (author's photograph).

PAGE 195 Caravaggio, detail from *The Calling of Saint Matthew*, Contarelli Chapel, Rome, Wikimedia Commons / CC-BY-SA-3.0 & GFDL.

PAGE 196 Siobhan Liddell, "Pentecost Petals in the Pantheon," 2012.

PAGE 199 Pieter Brueghel the Elder, detail from *The Tower of Babel* Wikimedia Commons / CC-BY-SA-3.0 & GFDL.

PAGE 201 Central nave, lower part inside porticus (Bern Digital Pantheon Project).

PAGE 203 Transport of Mussolini's monolith, 1929 (anonymous).

PAGE 206 Holger Weinandt, *Mülheim-Kärlich Nuclear Power Plant*, © Holger Weinandt / Wikimedia Commons / CC-BY-SA-3.0 & GFDL.

PAGE 207 Ralph Solonitz, *Examining the Don Drumm Sculpture* (courtesy of the May 4 Collection, Kent State University Libraries, Special Collections and Archives).

PAGE 209 Colin Gee, video still from *I, who am the chorus*, 2013.

PAGE 212 The Pantheon, with forecourt restored conjecturally, from *The Pantheon: Design, Meaning, and Progeny*, by William L. MacDonald (Penguin, 1976), © 1976 by William L. MacDonald. Reproduced by permission of Penguin Books Ltd.

PAGE 214 Staircase inside chambers (Bern Digital Pantheon Project).

PAGE 215 Frank Baker Holmes, staircase on the exterior of the Pantheon's dome.

PAGE 217 Frank Baker Holmes, solitary figure sitting near the Pantheon's oculus.

PAGE 219 Still from video entitled *9/11 WTC Tribute in Light Up-Close Showing Birds Trapped in the Light*, youtube.com.

PAGE 224 Annie Slizak, Fontana della Pigna in Cortile della Pigna, Vatican City, © Annie Slizak / Wikimedia Commons / CC-BY-SA-3.0 & GFDL.

Acknowledgments

⌒

Enormous gratitude is due to numerous people and organizations, without whom this book would not have been possible.

To the incredible staff of Trinity University Press, especially Sarah Nawrocki, for all her patient assistance, and Barbara Ras for her tremendous advocacy, enthusiasm, and steady guidance on my work.

To the artists and organizations who generously granted permission to reproduce the images on these pages, and to my pinch-hitting hodgepodge of friends who helped with translations and connections overseas.

To the editors of all of the journals where these essays first appeared, for their responses to my work and indispensable editorial suggestions.

To the Lannan Foundation for the beautiful gift of contiguous time during a Lannan Residency Fellowship that fostered several of these pieces. To the entire Lannan staff for all their assistance, especially Jo Chapman, who knew when time was needed most.

To the Whiting Foundation, for their extraordinary and generous support.

To Philip Levine, who steered me to Rome, and whose words seem to steer me every time I try to put words on the page.

To the Academy of Arts and Letters, who honored me with the staggering gift of a Rome Prize in Literature.

To the wonderful band of AAR Fellows who shared in the bliss of that year in Rome. To Brian Rose and all the AAR classical scholars who responded to my late-game exuberance with patience and vital expertise. To the entire American Academy in Rome staff—especially Giulia Barra, Adele Chapman, Karl Kirchwey, Pina Pasquantonio, and Cristina Puglisi—for their encouragement and tireless assistance, and for facilitating both my work and lark travels throughout Italy and Rome.

To Kathy Graber and Dana Levin, who buoyed me with friendship, feedback, and pitch-perfect edits on early drafts of many of these pieces.

To my parents, for their unwavering love and support.

To my tremendous kiddos, Cyrus and Oliver, for their tolerance, flare-ups of wonder, and general cheer as I hauled them to yet another backstreet Pompeii home or to the Pantheon's light once again.

And most of all, to Ligia—co-conspirator, guardian of my solitude, who somehow never failed to believe, and whose thoughts and insights fuel every page. This book could not be without you.

These essays first appeared in the following publications, sometimes in slightly different versions:

AGNI, "House of the Faun" and "Monkey Mind"

Black Warrior Review, "One Hundred and Twenty-One Seconds of Square Dance among Other Things"

Blackbird, "Almost a Full Year of Stone, Light, and Sky" (excerpt)

Cutbank, "House of the Vettii"

Kenyon Review, "Dew Point" and "Garden of the Fugitives"

PEN America, "Against Desire"

Seneca Review, "House of the Large Fountain"

Shadowgraph, "House of the Tragic Poet"

Threepenny Review, "Villa of the Mysteries"

Virginia Quarterly Review, "Leaving Trinity: Ten Ground Zero Swerves"

West Branch, "Toward Some Blossoms More or Less"

Matt Donovan is the author of *Vellum*, which received the 2008 Larry Levis Reading Prize from Virginia Commonwealth University, and the chapbook *Ten Burnt Lakes*. His work has appeared in numerous journals, including *AGNI, Blackbird, Kenyon Review, Seneca Review, Threepenny Review,* and *Virginia Quarterly Review*. He is the recipient of a Rome Prize in Literature, a Whiting Award, a Pushcart Prize, a National Endowment for the Arts Literature Fellowship, and a Lannan Writing Residency Fellowship. He is collaborating on a chamber opera with the artist Ligia Bouton, soprano Susan Narucki, and composer Lei Liang. Donovan teaches in the creative writing and literature department at Santa Fe University of Art and Design.